*YOUTH WITH DEPRESSION
AND ANXIETY*

Moods That
Overwhelm

HELPING YOUTH WITH MENTAL, PHYSICAL, AND SOCIAL CHALLENGES

Title List

Youth Coping with Teen Pregnancy:
Growing Up Fast

Youth Who Are Gifted:
Integrating Talents and Intelligence

Youth with Aggression Issues:
Bullying and Violence

Youth with Alcohol and Drug Addiction:
Escape from Bondage

Youth with Asperger's Syndrome:
A Different Drummer

Youth with Bipolar Disorder: Achieving Stability

Youth with Cancer: Facing the Shadows

Youth with Conduct Disorder:
In Trouble with the World

Youth with Cultural/Language Differences:
Interpreting an Alien World

Youth with Depression and Anxiety:
Moods That Overwhelm

Youth with Eating Disorders:
When Food Is an Enemy

Youth with Gender Issues: Seeking an Identity

Youth with HIV/AIDS: Living with the Diagnosis

Youth with Impulse-Control Disorders:
On the Spur of the Moment

Youth with Juvenile Schizophrenia:
The Search for Reality

YOUTH WITH DEPRESSION
AND ANXIETY

Moods That Overwhelm

by Kenneth McIntosh
and Phyllis Livingston

Mason Crest Publishers
Philadelphia

Mason Crest Publishers Inc.
370 Reed Road
Broomall, Pennsylvania 19008
(866) MCP-BOOK (toll free)
www.masoncrest.com

First printing

1 2 3 4 5 6 7 8 9 10

ISBN 978-1-4222-0133-6 (series)

Library of Congress Cataloging-in-Publication Data

McIntosh, Kenneth, 1959–
  Youth with depression and anxiety : moods that overwhelm / by Kenneth McIntosh and Phyllis Livingston.
    p. cm. — (Helping youth with mental, physical, and
social challenges)
  Includes bibliographical references and index.
  ISBN 978-1-4222-0142-8
  1. Depression in adolescence—Juvenile literature. I. Livingston, Phyllis, 1957– II. Title.
RJ506.D4M332 2008
618.92'8527—dc22
                                        2006022378

Interior pages produced by
Harding House Publishing Service, Inc.
www.hardinghousepages.com
Interior design by MK Bassett-Harvey.
Cover design by MK Bassett-Harvey.
Cover Illustration by Keith Rosko.
Printed in the Hashemite Kingdom of Jordan.

The creators of this book have made every effort to provide
accurate information, but it should not be used as a substitute for
the help and services of trained professionals.

Contents

Introduction **6**

1. Stacie's Grave **9**

2. Fired **23**

3. Josh **39**

4. Hope **59**

5. Into the Abyss **79**

6. On Waking **95**

7. Drowning **105**

8. New Beginnings **115**

Glossary **120**

Further Reading **122**

For More Information **123**

Bibliography **124**

Index **125**

Picture Credits **127**

Author and Consultant Biographies **128**

1679

Introduction

We are all people first, before anything else. Our shared humanity is more important than the impressions we give to each other by how we look, how we learn, or how we act. Each of us is worthy simply because we are all part of the human race. Though we are all different in many ways, we can celebrate our differences as well as our similarities.

In this book series, you will read about many young people with various special needs that impact their lives in different ways. The disabilities are not *who* the people are, but the disabilities are an important characteristic of each person. When we recognize that we all have differing needs, we can grow toward greater awareness and tolerance of each other. Just as important, we can learn to accept our differences.

Not all young people with a disability are the same as the persons in the stories. But you will learn from these stories how a special need impacts a young person, as well as his or her family and friends. The story will help you understand differences better and appreciate how differences make us all stronger and better.

—*Cindy Croft, M.A.Ed.*

Did you know that as many as 8 percent of teens experience anxiety or depression, and as many as 70 to 90 percent will use substances such as alcohol or illicit drugs at some time? Other young people are living with life-threatening diseases including HIV infection and cancer, as well as chronic psychiatric conditions such as bipolar disease and schizophrenia. Still other teens have the challenge of being "different" from peers because they are intellectually gifted, are from another culture, or have trouble controlling their behavior or socializing with others. All youth with challenges experience additional stresses compared to their typical peers. The good news is that there are many resources and supports available to help these young people, as well as their friends and families.

The stories contained in each book of this series also contain factual information that will enhance your own understanding of the particular condition being presented. If you or someone you know is struggling with a similar condition or experience, this series can give you important information about where and how you can get help. After reading these stories, we hope that you will be more open to the differences you encounter in your peers and more willing to get to know others who are "different."

—*Carolyn Bridgemohan, M.D.*

Chapter 1
Stacie's Grave

tacie, I miss you so much. . . . I wish I could just call you on your cell and hear you pick up. We used to talk about everything, and now I need someone to talk to in the worst way."

The lone living figure in the tomb-studded expanse of Shepherd's Rest Cemetery, Ashley huddled over her friend's grave. Right now, she should be in fifth-period class, with Miss Cuevas drilling them on Spanish verb endings, but Ashley could barely stand being in school these days. Yesterday, she started to freak out during first period; her chest went so tight she could barely suck in a breath, and she had to excuse herself to the bathroom for fear she was going to scream. This morning, she had felt so weak and bleak she knew she couldn't make it through a day of classes. Instead, she drove up the winding hills to Shepherd's Rest, where she could talk with her best friend—even though her friend was dead.

"Stacie, I'm so sorry I didn't understand what you were going through. I would have listened. . . . I should have been a better friend."

They had been friends since second grade, when they were in the same ballet class. That was when both of them had a mom and dad at home, and in the afternoons they played with Barbie dolls and watched *Where in the World Is Carmen Sandiego?* As they got older, though, life got darker. Both their families broke up; Stacie lived with her mom, a situation that was okay for her, but Ashley wound up with her dad, and she couldn't imagine a worse fate. Nonetheless, Ashley and Stacie had some good times in their junior high years. The two girls went to Surf Camp together, and they took to the ocean like a pair of pint-sized mermaids. By freshman year in high school, they could pull stunts on their boards that made some of the guys at Marina High jealous.

Then, two years ago, Stacie started changing. She would be unhappy for long stretches of time, too tired to go any-where, talking listlessly about how grim her life was; she lost interest in surfing, flirting with boys, and other activities. The two remained friends, but it was increasingly difficult for Ashley to enjoy Stacie's company; she was always so down.

Stacie talked about the medications she was taking and how she hoped she would feel better soon. For a couple of weeks, it even looked as though Stacie's wishes had been granted. By the start of fall semester, Stacie's behavior had changed from one extreme to another! She was bright and bubbly and loud and crazy, as insanely outgoing and wild as she had been sad and withdrawn. Ashley had thought this new side to her friend was a lot of fun, but she had sometimes feared Stacie was getting out of hand. She was doing dangerous things, like going out with boys she hardly knew and partying wildly on the weekends. Her manic spree lasted almost a month—and then darkness clouded over Stacie again. She withdrew from the Marina High social scene and settled into her old depression. She came home from school exhausted, and some days stayed home to sleep. Ashley had feared for her friend.

Then one terrible day, Mrs. Leone, the school counselor, called Ashley and a handful of others into her office. They sat, silent, wondering what this meeting could be about. Mrs. Leone told them a lifeguard had found Stacie's body in the water that morning. Stacie was dead.

Officially, Stacie died of accidental drowning, but Ashley didn't believe it: she was sure her friend had committed suicide. Stacie's mom thought the same; she kept talking to people in the medical field and finally surmised that Stacie had been suffering from what they called bipolar mood disorder, an illness that causes people who have it to swing back and forth between depression and mania. She was convinced her daughter had been given the wrong medications, resulting in her death.

Now, bending over her friend's grave, Ashley spoke softly. "Stacie, I remember all those days when you were so down. I used to get mad when you couldn't say anything happy, when you wouldn't get off the sofa or out of your bed. I'm sorry now, because I understand. You were depressed—your body felt tired and heavy every day, so you didn't want to get out of the house. You could only see darkness . . . only feel despair." Ashley choked back a sob in her throat.

"I've been feeling that same way, for months now. It totally sucks being me. I hate myself. I don't like the way I look, I hate trying to talk to Dad because he's always drinking at night and he never listens or understands me. Life just seems so empty; I feel helpless." Ashley lay down on her friend's grave, allowing herself to rest on the grass as if she were embracing her departed friend.

"Dad took me to see our family doctor, but the guy's a jerk—he listened to me for like five minutes and wrote a prescription. He says I have 'depression mixed with anxiety," that I just have to take these pills and everything will be fine. Yeah, right. I've been taking the drugs for a month now, but it doesn't feel like anything is changing. I'm scared taking those pills . . . what if they just make me worse?" *Like you.* Ashley couldn't bring herself to say the words out loud.

Ashley sat up and removed her shades, wiping her eyes with the sleeves of her shirt. She looked out over the golden foothills surrounding the cemetery and glanced at the wispy traces of clouds in the bright blue sky. Then she turned and looked at her friend's gravestone, and read the words again:

> *Stacie King*
> *1989–2005*
> *Beloved Daughter and Friend*
> *Free now from all your pain*

That last phrase seemed to reach out to Ashley, grabbing hold of her mind. "Free now from all your pain. . . ." she whispered the words several times, as though they held a secret message.

"Stacie, I miss you but . . . I kind of envy you, too. I'm tired of feeling down all the time. It gets harder and harder going to school and work. I'm afraid something really bad will happen. I'm lonely. There's no one I really trust. I don't have any friends left at school, Dad won't listen, the doctor is worthless. . . . I'm trapped, and scared, and I hate it."

Ashley closed her eyes and lifted her face toward the sun, then looked back down at her friend's gravestone.

"You're free now, from all your pain. I wish I could be free from mine."

She paused, then whispered to her friend, "Maybe I'll come join you soon, wherever you are. Then I'll be free, too."

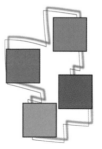

What Are Moods?

A mood is a temporary state of mind or emotion. Normally, our moods **fluctuate** from day to day, and even from hour to hour. When our moods become overwhelming, though, or fluctuate wildly, then that is not normal and may be an indication that we are experiencing a **mood disorder**.

People often think of their moods as something separate from their physical bodies, but actually, our emotions have physical causes. They are produced by chemicals and other activity in our brains.

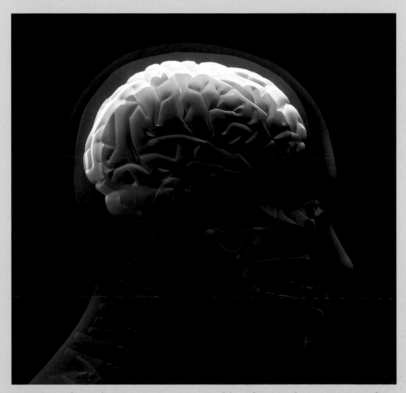

Our moods and emotions are caused by chemical activities in the brain.

In 2002, scientists at Vanderbilt University scanned healthy people's brains and found that people who reported having been in a bad mood recently had increased activity in a region of the brain called the ventromedial prefrontal cortex, which lies an inch or two behind the right eye in right-handed people; other studies have also linked this area with emotions. This region of the brain also controls heart rate, breathing, stomach acid levels, sweating, and similar body functions known to have close connections to mood.

What Is Depression?

Depression is one of the most common major mood disorders and involves changes in a person's emotions, behavior, and thought patterns, changes that are strong enough to disrupt a person's usual functioning for six months or more. Depression impacts the way a person feels about himself, how he thinks, and even how he eats and sleeps. Although depression may seem like a temporary "down-in-the-dumps" mood, the person who is depressed cannot simply "cheer up" after a while. Depression is a disorder over which the person has no control. Some symptoms of depression include:

- feelings of extreme sadness, emptiness, anxiety
- thoughts of hopelessness, helplessness
- thoughts of suicide, suicide attempts
- loss of interest in usual activities, such as hobbies, school, or work
- loss of appetite or overeating

It is normal for a person's moods to vary from day to day, or even hour to hour. However, if her emotions become overwhelming, or moods fluctuate wildly, she may have a mood disorder.

- oversleeping or waking up unusually early, and difficulty sleeping
- loss of concentration, difficulty remembering
- fatigue
- restlessness or irritability
- physical symptoms such as headaches, backaches, and digestive trouble that do not improve with medical treatment

Not everyone who is depressed experiences all of these symptoms, however. According to the *Diagnostic and Statistical Manual for Mental Disorders, Fourth Edition* (DSM-IV), a person must display from at least five of the above symptoms. Everyone gets sad now and then, but unlike a usual "blue" mood, the symptoms of depression may last for weeks, months, or even, in some cases, years. A person with depression typically experiences depressive episodes, periods during which she is depressed, several times over the course of her life.

What Is Anxiety?

Merriam-Webster's 11th Collegiate Dictionary has two definitions for the word anxiety. The first is "painful or apprehensive uneasiness of mind usually over an impending or anticipated ill"—while the second is somewhat different: "an abnormal and overwhelming sense of apprehension and fear often marked by physiological signs (such as sweating, tension, and increased pulse), by doubt concerning the reality and nature of the threat, and by self-doubt about one's capacity to cope with it."

Almost everyone feels that first type of anxiety now and then, so it's important to distinguish between anxiety disorders and normal anxiety. In her book *Mental Health Concepts and Techniques*, Mary Beth Early defines the everyday, run-of-the-mill sort of anxiety as a state of tension and uneasiness. Anxious feelings from time to time are normal, even useful, parts of daily life.

Sometimes anxious feelings can result from simple physical causes, such as eating and drinking things that contain caffeine or large quantities of sugar. Tobacco and alcohol can also cause changes in anxiety levels.

Anxiety can even be a positive thing that helps us to avoid harm. After all, anxiety may make us fear the consequences of not checking the kitchen when we smell smoke, of not studying for an exam, or of not paying our taxes to the IRS. Anxious feelings can help get us ready to face difficulties or challenges, and sometimes even emergencies. Walter B. Cannon, an American physiologist, was the first to identify what he called the "fight-or-flight" reaction, our body's response to emergency situations. This response includes a sudden increase in heart rate, breathing rate, and blood pressure, and also an increase in

One symptom of depression is a loss of interest in normal activities, such as school, work, or social life.

blood flow to muscles. These physical changes are all meant to allow a person to either flee or fight in the face of danger.

Performing artists recognize that a little anxiety helps put an "edge" on a performance, driving the artist to do a bit better than would be possible without

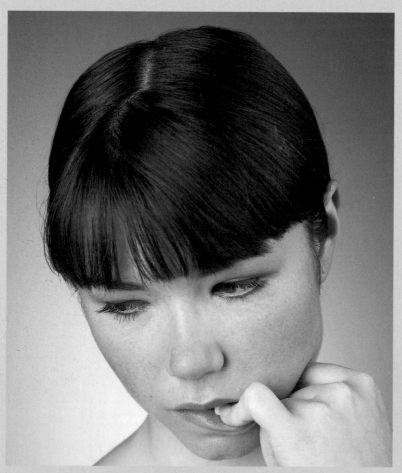

Everyone gets worried or anxious sometimes. In fact, a little anxiety may actually improve a test grade, give an edge to a performance, or help you survive an emergency situation.

it. Now, scientific measurements of blood flow in the brain using modern brain-imaging techniques show that low levels of anxiety cause an increase in brain activity. Students who are a *little* worried about an upcoming test actually have a better ability to concentrate and retain information. Large amounts of anxiety have just the opposite effect on the brain, however. Some people talk about "freezing up" when they take a test or give a speech, and that may be an apt expression, since brain activity seems to decrease in the presence of excessive anxiety.

Unlike these reasonable kinds of worry, which are linked to specific situations such as performance or possible danger, anxiety disorders involve anxious feelings for which there is apparently no reason at all. In psychiatric terms, this abnormal state of anxiety is characterized by the feeling of powerlessness and the inability to cope with threatening events, typically imaginary, and by physical tension evidenced by sweating, trembling, and other **physiological** reactions.

Since nearly everyone experiences anxious feelings at one time or another, some people assume that an anxiety disorder is not a serious condition. But if anxious feelings grow so strong that they interfere with daily functioning at work, school, or in relationships, and if this problem lasts for six months or more, it is important to seek professional help. True anxiety disorders can be very serious and, at times, **incapacitating** for many people.

Chapter 2
Fired

t was a crazy night at Sandy's Pier-End Café, and Ashley was struggling to keep up with her job. Music blared from a vintage jukebox, barely audible above noisy conversations. Local teens, fishermen, and tourists enjoying a taste of the Southern California beach scene filled the red-and-white checkered tables and waited in line outside on the pier.

Although Ashley disliked her own appearance, for some reason customers at Sandy's always seemed to think she looked pretty, flying from table to table with an order pad or plates of hot food in her hands. Sometimes, boys would ask for her number, but Ashley just gave them a dirty look;

she couldn't think about anything but surviving the night and keeping her job.

When she was first hired, Ashley enjoyed her job at Sandy's, but now she dreaded her work there so much that she had called in sick several nights recently. Ashley knew her boss wasn't happy with her, but every time she went to work, she had to battle the waves of panic that swept over her. Sometimes, she felt so anxious that all she could hear was her heart pounding. It was getting so she hated to leave home at all. When she was in her own room, she was so sad she could barely move—but that was better than leaving the house and being overwhelmed by such an enormous tidal wave of panic.

"Waitress, I ordered the Maui Burger, not this . . . whatever it is."

"I'm sorry, ma'am, the kitchen must have made a mistake, I'll get it fixed right away." Ashley couldn't tell if she was whispering or shouting; all she could hear was the *thump-thump-thump* of her own heart.

"Young lady, we've been waiting an hour for our shakes. It doesn't take more than a minute to mix them up. We're about ready to walk outta here. Where are those shakes?"

"Sorry, folks, uh . . . I'll check back at the kitchen right away." Her hands were shaking so much that she hid them in her apron where no one would see.

"Hey! Surfer chick, where ya been lately?"

That one stopped Ashley dead in her tracks. She turned to face a table of her classmates, tanned and toned, clad in long trunks and tank tops, looking like they just came in from playing in the ocean.

She paused, trying to think of her answer. She couldn't very well tell them that her life hurt all over, that she was too scared to leave her house unless she really had to, that she felt like crying all the time, that she didn't have enough energy to cope with the panic she felt whenever she went to work or school, let alone the extra oomph she would have needed to go carve up waves. In fact, she hadn't surfed since Stacie's drowning.

As she struggled to find words, Ashley suddenly felt dizzy. She tried once, twice, to take a breath, but couldn't seem to draw air into her lungs. *Oh no*, she was having a full-fledged panic attack, the last thing she needed on a busy night.

"Ashley! Get in here—now!" It was the short-order cook calling from the kitchen. Ashley turned and stumbled through the kitchen door, then leaned back against a refrigerator, steadying herself. Her words seemed to come from far away, but she heard herself say, "Just a minute, Mario— I'll be right with you." Then she turned and walked into the bathroom.

Without bothering to turn on the lights, she sat down on a closed toilet and put her face in her hands. She felt as though she couldn't get a full breath of air, and she was trembling all over. Then the door flew open; she had forgotten to lock it.

Another waitress, Suzie, stood framed in the bright light of the kitchen. Her eyes adjusted to the dark room and she saw Ashley, sitting on the stool, gasping for breath. Suzie looked shocked for a moment, then ran back into the kitchen, calling "Mrs. Beemer—something's wrong with Ashley!"

"Oh no! Don't call the boss" Ashley gasped. Her manager, Mrs. Beemer, opened the door, turned on the light, and looked at Ashley. Their relationship of late had not been very good, so Ashley expected little sympathy.

"Ashley, the tables are a mess—there are half a dozen customers yelling for you. What is going on?"

Ashley tried to open her mouth, but her vocal chords wouldn't move. She felt dizzy again, short of breath, as though a huge clammy hand had grabbed hold of her insides. Ashley grasped on to the grab bar beside the toilet, steadying herself, staring at her boss like a deer in the headlights of a Mack truck.

Mrs. Beemer stared silently at the frightened waitress, sizing up the situation. Then she said quietly, "Ashley, I'm sorry, but every night your performance on the job gets worse and I've put up with your problems long enough. I'm letting you go. You can pick up your final check on Monday."

Mrs. Beemer closed the door, and Ashley was alone. She sat there a few more minutes until she could control herself, then stood up and walked out of the bathroom, through the kitchen, and out onto the pier. *Life always seems darkest just before it goes pitch black,* she thought to herself.

She walked down the length of the pier from the restaurant to the mainland, shivering a little in her Sandy's miniskirt. There were always interesting things to see on the pier: outrageously dressed tourists from around the world, local students hanging out with their skateboards, and fishermen hauling in bizarre catches from the waters beneath the barnacled pylons. Tonight, however, Ashley just stared at the wooden planks in front of her feet, her mood shifting from panic to despair. What would she do now to pay for her car? Her dad insisted she pay her own gas and insurance, and she bought most of her own clothes. She couldn't imagine how she was going to pay for these necessities, but she was frightened thinking of finding and keeping another job.

Her old Toyota was parked in the public lot next to the pier. She climbed inside and headed for home. On the way, she thought to herself, *Please, please let Dad be in a decent mood . . . just this once. I can't deal with him tonight. I just can't.*

She turned her car into the drive, turned off the lights, and sat for a long minute. Again, she felt the edgy sense of fear rising up within her, like some angry beast with talons squeezing her chest. She shut her eyes, tried to breathe slowly, then forced her body out of the car. It seemed as if lead weights hung from her arms and legs; it was hard to move.

When she came into the living room, she found her father sitting on the sofa, watching the tube; five empty beer cans cluttered the coffee table, and another one was in her father's hand.

"What are you doing home so early?"

Ashley tried to pull some appropriate response out of her sluggish mind.

"What's wrong? Why don't you speak up?"

She opened her mouth, but no words came. He stared at her, and then he grunted, "Don't tell me you got fired?!"

As long as Ashley could remember, her father had had an amazing talent to detect her embarrassing mistakes and failures. She hung her head as his voice became louder. "Ashley, of all the stupid things to do! Who's going to pay for your insurance? Your gas? Not me! That's for sure. You have to grow up and be responsible."

She stumbled toward the staircase, grasped the railing, and pulled her weary body upward as her father's angry ramblings continued in the room below. When she finally reached her room, her refuge, she slammed the door and leaned her back against it. Her father was shouting up the staircase.

"You better shape up Ashley, you hear? You're getting into more and more trouble. The school called . . . you've been cutting classes! And now you get fired? What's wrong with you?"

Ashley wanted to yell back at him, to say, "At least I'm not an alcoholic like you are—at least I live my miserable life without drowning in booze every night like you do!" But she didn't have the energy inside; she felt smothered by a thick blanket of weariness and pain. She fell face forward on her bed and put a pillow over her ears to silence her father's angry voice.

Lying in the dark, Ashley wondered, *How long before the sadness and panic just swallow me up completely? Maybe it isn't worth the effort to go on living.*

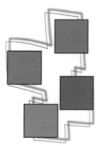

The Diagnostic and Statistical Manual of Mental Disorders, fourth edition (DSM-IV) describes several varieties of anxiety that are more than just worried feelings. These are true psychiatric disorders that need professional attention.

Generalized Anxiety Disorder (GAD)

GAD is a type of excessive anxiety that lasts for at least six months, more days than not, with no reasonable cause. It may occur even when the sufferer's life is going very well. GAD may include **chronic** feelings of restlessness, difficulty concentrating, tiring easily, irritability, muscle tension, and difficulty in sleeping.

Individuals with GAD find it difficult to control their worry, are distressed by their condition, and find the anxiety they feel keeps them from functioning as well as they otherwise could in their work, school, or social situations. The things they worry about are everyday, routine life circumstances including finances, health (their own or that of family members), misfortune to children, job responsibilities (present or anticipated), household chores, and car repairs. Children who suffer from GAD typically worry about their own ability to perform, particularly in areas such as school or sporting events, and about catastrophic events including war, terrorist attacks, or earthquakes. During the time an individual has GAD, worry may shift from one concern to another. More women than men are diagnosed with GAD.

People with GAD frequently experience aches and pains, such as stomachache, backache, and headache. For females, menstrual cramps are included.

Trembling, twitching, and "feeling shaky" are also reported, as well as sweating, nausea, diarrhea, and an exaggerated **startle response**.

Often, people with GAD have felt anxious or nervous for their entire lives, but onset of GAD after age twenty is not unusual. People who are generally more anxious than others often come from families where this trait is **prevalent**.

Panic Disorder

Panic disorder is a kind of anxiety distinguished by recurrent, unexpected panic attacks, followed by a persistent concern (which lasts for a minimum of one month) about having another panic attack. A

An individual with GAD is excessively worried, all the time, about everyday things, such as school and homework.

panic attack is defined as a period of intense fear or discomfort where specific symptoms, which develop suddenly and reach a peak within ten minutes, are present. These symptoms include the following:

- palpitations (rapid beating or fluttering of the heart), pounding heart
- accelerated heart rate
- sweating
- trembling or shaking
- sensations of shortness of breath/smothering
- feeling of choking
- chest pain or discomfort
- nausea/abdominal distress
- feeling dizzy, unsteady, light-headed, or faint
- derealization (feelings of unreality) or depersonalization (detachment from self)
- fear of losing control or going crazy
- fear of dying
- parasthesias (numbness or tingling sensations)
- chills or hot flashes

According to the DSM-IV, a minimum of four of these symptoms must be present to qualify an episode as a panic attack.

People with panic disorder often fear that their attacks indicate they have some undiagnosed, life-threatening disease, and they may be unconvinced by medical tests that show this is not the case. Such fears may lead the individual to make repeated

Someone in the middle of a panic attack may have trouble breathing, start sweating profusely, and feel dizzy, among other symptoms.

visits to doctors and emergency rooms—even to the extent of missing so much work that their jobs are endangered. Individuals with this disorder may also be far less tolerant of medication side effects; they may require repeated reassurances in order to continue taking their medication. Other people fear their panic attacks mean they are losing their minds or they are emotionally weak.

Disruptions in interpersonal relationships, such as leaving home to live independently or getting a divorce, may bring on (or significantly worsen) panic disorder. When this happens, many individuals become discouraged or unhappy about carrying on with their normal routines; they may consider this a sign of a personal lack of strength or character. In some cases, people even respond to panic attacks by significantly changing their behavior or situation. This may mean, for example, that they quit their jobs, avoid all physical exertion, or move their residences.

Panic attacks may occur with or without agoraphobia.

Panic Attack with Agoraphobia

This multisyllable word is easier to understand if you break it down into two pieces: *agora* and *phobia*. In ancient Greece, the "agora" was a large, open place where people could assemble, particularly a

An individual with agoraphobia may be afraid to venture outside her own home.

marketplace. And according to Webster's Dictionary, "phobia" means an irrational, excessive, persistent fear of a thing or a situation. The word "agoraphobia" is formed by combining these two words, and Webster's Dictionary defines it as an abnormal fear of being in open or public places.

The essential feature of agoraphobia is an anxiety about being in places or situations from which one might not be able to escape without difficulty or where help might not be available in case of a panic attack (or related symptoms such as dizziness or diarrhea). This fear involves being outside one's home alone and often includes being in crowds, standing in lines, being on a bridge, or traveling in a bus, train, or automobile.

Some individuals with agoraphobia venture into such situations but endure intense distress while doing so. Some tolerate such excursions better when they have a companion along, while others find leaving the house all but impossible.

Phobia

A specific phobia is an excessive or unreasonable fear that a person experiences when in the presence of the feared object or situation, a fear that interferes with the individual's normal functioning. This fear is usually related to the harm the individual anticipates from the object or situation. For instance, many people have phobias about flying in airplanes because they fear what could happen if the airplane crashed. Other people fear dogs (or other animals) because they anticipate the possibility of being bitten or otherwise attacked.

Another type of specific phobia involves fear of losing control, panicking, or fainting in response to blood, injury, heights, elevators, and so on. Several of the specific phobias have become well known by their names (and at least one has been used as a movie title):

- **arachnophobia:** fear of spiders
- **claustrophobia:** fear of closed-in spaces
- **coulrophobia:** fear of clowns
- **triscadekophobia:** fear of Friday the thirteenth.

Phobia is not diagnosed when an individual experiences a reasonable fear, such as if someone is concerned about being shot when in a dangerous neighborhood or fears a car accident while driving on a crowded, six-lane freeway.

Specific phobia is divided into several subtypes for diagnostic purposes, and the subtypes give an indication of the most common phobias, with the feared objects, places, or situations (known as triggers) in parentheses. Subtypes include:

- animal type (animals or insects)
- natural environment type (storms, heights, water)
- blood-injection/injury type (seeing blood, injury, receiving injections, or undergoing other medical procedures)
- situational type (public transportation, tunnels, bridges, elevators, flying, driving, enclosed places)
- other type (choking, vomiting; also includes "space" phobia—fear of falling down if

away from walls or other means of support;
children's fears of characters in costumes or
of loud noises)

Specific phobias may be triggered or contributed
to by actual **traumatic** events, such as choking,
being trapped in a closet or other small space, or dog
bites. Other contributing factors to specific phobia
can include observing people in a traumatic situation
and hearing frequent warnings from parents about
the dangers of certain objects or situations.

Social Phobia

Social phobia is an individual's overwhelming and
disabling fear of either social or performance situations
where she may be embarrassed or humiliated.
Exposure to the feared situation usually provokes an
anxiety response, which may take the form of a panic
attack. The individual (except in the case of children)
realizes the fear is unreasonable or excessive and is
distressed by having it.

For people with social phobia, common responses
in social or performance situations may include
palpitations, tremors, sweating, gastrointestinal
discomfort, diarrhea, muscle tension, blushing, and
confusion. The overriding concern seems to be that
others will notice that the sufferer's hands or voices
tremble in such situations, or that she will appear
inarticulate, leading other people to consider her
weak, crazy, stupid, or anxious. Due to this fear,
individuals with social phobia may stop eating,
drinking, or writing in public. They will find that their
phobia interferes substantially with their functioning
at school, work, or in other social settings.

Chapter 3
Josh

onday came, and Ashley had to cope with another day at school. Lately, she had withdrawn from her old circle of acquaintances. She felt nervous around groups of people, and she lacked the energy to engage in the Marina High social scene. She ignored her peers, and for the most part, her peers ignored her in return; it was as though she and her classmates were ghosts passing through one another without really touching. But despite her best efforts, she couldn't completely avoid interactions with her peers. Some unpleasant encounters were inevitable.

Walking in the hallway between third and fourth period, Ashley passed a group of girls gathered in front of the central staircase, clustered around Vanna Khan. Vanna was someone Ashley preferred not to see, as she highlighted Ashley's feelings of inadequacy. Every week Vanna dressed in at least one new outfit, the sort of clothes sold in expensive Laguna stores; her hair was always meticulously arranged, and to top it off, her parents had paid for a boob job as a gift for her sixteenth birthday (a reminder for Ashley that she had not been invited to Vanna's sweet sixteen party—though seemingly every other kid at Marina had been).

As Ashley walked by, Vanna called out to her. "Oh, Ashley, I am sooo sorry!"

"Huh?" Ashley stopped and stared at Vanna.

"About your little incident at Sandy's—how you lost your job. Is everything all right, hon?"

Vanna's use of the word "hon" had all the sincerity of a cat waiting to pounce on a hapless mouse. Ashley glared at her and chose to move on without answering. Behind her, she heard one of Vanna's friends murmuring, "I heard she just *lost* it. Poor thing, she is totally going mental."

Part of Ashley wanted to yell back at the girls and tell them what rich, stuck-up idiots they all were; but then, another part of her agreed with them. Yep, that was her all right: Ashley the nut case, depressed and nervous all the time, failing at school, failing socially, failing at work, failing every way you looked. She felt the tears swelling up and decided she wasn't ready to face her next class.

She cut out of the back door from the main building and headed for a little alcove with a bench seat surrounded by large, leafy bird of paradise plants. She needed to sit alone for the hour, working up courage to go to her next class. Her head in her hands, she tried to stop trembling, to regain control. She breathed in and out slowly, silently crying out to no one in particular for help: *Getting through the fear is so hard every day. I need to believe my life is worth living.*

Sha-clunk! It was the familiar sound of a skateboard rolling to a stop and being flipped up by the rider's foot. Out the side of her eye, Ashley saw a pair of baggy shorts and well-tanned feet in Tevas. She looked up: it was Josh Bruner, whom some Marina girls jokingly referred to as "Boy Wonder." The nickname did not denote any disrespect: Josh was popular yet he managed to befriend geeks and misfits without losing his reputation. He was ripped, he wore muscle shirts, and his long blond hair hung down his back in a ponytail, but he nonetheless carried respect not usually given to the tie-dye-soul-surfer crowd. Part of his reputation was the aura of calm detachment he always displayed, cool and wise like some Zen monk.

"Okay if I join you?"

Ashley looked up, her eyes wet, and nodded. Josh plopped his six-foot frame down on the bench beside her, shaking the wooden seat.

"Haven't seen you in the water for a while."

Ashley stared at the ground and said nothing.

"I remember last year, you were really shredding out there. You were the hottest thing in Surf City tearing up those waves."

"Yeah," Ashley said, "But. . ." Her throat closed up, and she couldn't finish the sentence.

"I know." Josh picked up the thought for her. "It isn't the same without Stacie. I miss her a lot."

His words uncorked the bottle full of painful emotions Ashley had been trying to keep stoppered. She started shaking and sobbing.

Josh sat beside her, waiting for her to calm down before he spoke again.

"You've been feeling pretty bad lately, huh?"

"Uh-huh."

"I don't see you smile much these days."

"Nope."

"Listen, Ashley, I suppose it's none of my business, but I have to say something. A lot of us were worried about Stacie, but we didn't know how to help her. She was in real pain, but we were all too busy, or too selfish, or too absorbed with our own issues to say anything—until it was too late."

Once again, Ashley felt her emotional dam bursting. Josh had to wait a few more minutes before she stopped crying again. Then he continued. "Ashley, I . . . I've always liked being around you." She glanced at him, trying to interpret this remark. "You're special. Really. But I'm worried about you. I know you're really down. I want to say something to you while . . . at a time when maybe it will help." His voice was so low now she could barely hear him. "I don't want to make the same mistake I made with Stacie."

"What are you, Josh, some kind of counselor now?"

He ignored the remark and went on. "You know my sister, Andrea?"

"Yeah."

"She's struggled a lot over the last few years with depression. So I've learned a few things about it by watching her."

"You mean she's screwed up? Like I am?"

Josh shook his head, still gazing at Ashley's face with his big blue eyes. "She's not screwed up, and neither are you, not anymore than someone with a cold or pneumonia. Depression is a disease that drags down your mind and your body—but you can get better. I've watched Andrea go through hell, but she got help and she's okay now."

"Yeah, well I saw a doctor, and he gave me pills—a lot of good they're doing me. Stacie was on meds too, and her mom thinks they killed her."

Josh nodded. "There are some bad doctors out there, but there are more good doctors. Really. My sister sees a psychiatrist, Dr. Graham. She's cool. She helped Andrea turn her life around. Let me give you this, in case you want to call her." He offered Ashley a business card imprinted with the words:

> *Dr. Monica Graham, Psychiatrist*
> *Redondo Medical Group,*
> *Specialist in Emotional Disorders*

Josh waited until Ashley took the card from his fingers. "I bet she could help you, and I really think you'd like her."

Ashley shook her head. "My dad would have to pay for treatments, and he wouldn't want to. He doesn't understand. Besides, I don't even care anymore."

Josh nodded as though he understood what she was really saying. "You're afraid it will just hurt worse if you fail. But you have to keep trying. I remember you hitting a set of big waves, diving right through those monster swells. Everyone was watching you, saying, 'That chick has guts!' Well you're still the same girl you were then. You can deal with this illness, Ashley—you can beat it."

Josh stood up, kicked his skateboard flat, and stepped onto it. He rolled a few feet, then stopped and turned back. "Ashley, Stacie was my friend too. I think I know what she'd say if she were here right now. She'd tell you to fight, not to let this thing defeat you." He turned, shoved off with one foot, and went clacking down the sidewalk.

Ashley sat still for several minutes, alone with the bird of paradise plants. A silent debate raged within her head, a tug-of-war between her everyday sense of despair and the hope of a better tomorrow.

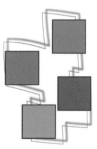

Whom Does Depression Affect?

Depression may occur in the young and old, both male and female. According to the National Institute of Mental Health, as many as 20.9 million adults in the United States may suffer from depression in a given year. That is 9.5 percent of the total population. The National Institute of Mental Health estimates depression affects about twelve million women and between six and seven million men.

According to the Mood Disorders Society of Canada, between 7.9 percent and 8.6 percent of the

Depression can affect anyone, of any age or sex. According to NIMH, in any given year, about 9.5 percent of the total population of the United States might be struggling with depression.

Canadian population will suffer from depression at some point in their lives. During any twelve-month period, the Society reports that between 4 percent and 5 percent of the population are experiencing major depression.

Depression in adolescents may be difficult to detect because the symptoms can hide behind emotional, behavioral, and physical changes typically associated with adolescence. However, excessive sleeping and moodiness, an uncharacteristic loss of interest in school, and thoughts of suicide are all symptoms of depression that should be taken seriously.

Whom Does Anxiety Affect?

Anxiety disorders are the single most common psychiatric illness in North America. Estimates are that at least 18 percent of all Americans suffer from an anxiety disorder in any given year. Anxiety disorders affect an estimated 13 percent of children and adolescents during any given six-month period, making them the most common class of psychiatric disorders in that age group. The Mood Disorders Society of Canada reports that 12 percent of the population suffers from anxiety disorders causing mild to severe impairment of their daily lives.

Social phobia is the third most common psychiatric disorder in the United States and afflicts about 15 million people each year. It usually begins in the mid-teens, sometimes in a person who has a childhood history of shyness. At other times it may follow an especially stressful or embarrassing experience, and it can last throughout a person's life, growing more and less prevalent according to his life circumstances.

Many anxiety disorders are more common in women than in men, and the tendency to experience serious anxiety seems to run in families. Panic disorder without agoraphobia, for example, is diagnosed twice as often in women as in men; with agoraphobia, it is diagnosed three times as often in women. The most typical age of onset of panic disorder is between

Many anxiety disorders are more common in women than in men.

late adolescence and the mid-thirties, although even children and people over age forty-five can experience the onset of this disorder. There appears to be a genetic factor in panic disorder, as indicated by a higher incidence in immediate family members of those with the disorder, and by **twin studies**.

What Causes Depression?

The cause of depression has eluded scientists for more than fifty years; however, scientists today emphasize that more than one, if not several factors, may cause depression. The likelihood that a person will experience depression is determined by interactions between a person's biology, psychology, and environment. Several factors may influence the probability that an individual will develop depression:

- genetics
- social or environmental conditions
- thought patterns
- insecure attachments
- physical conditions such as illness
- individual vulnerability and stress

A family history of depression may make someone more vulnerable or predisposed to developing the disorder. In other words, some physical changes in the brain associated with depression can sometimes be passed down genetically from one generation to the next. However, not all people with a genetic vulnerability to depression develop the disorder, just as people without a genetic vulnerability to depression may nevertheless experience depression.

Twin studies indicate that there is a genetic factor involved in the development of panic disorder.

Social theories on the cause of depression focus on stressful events in a person's life. A person who experiences violent or traumatic situations may be more susceptible to developing depression. Other stressful situations such as the loss of a job or financial difficulties may increase the likelihood of having depression. However, these theories do not account for people who lead safe and secure lives but nevertheless develop depression, nor do they explain why most people who experience violence or trauma do not suffer from depression.

In some cases, a person's thinking habits may make her more likely to develop depression. This **cognitive** theory of depression focuses on three **pessimistic** ways of thinking:

- internality
- stability
- lack of control

A person whose thinking habits show internality believes the reason for her unhappiness is inside herself. For example, she may think, "No one wants to talk to me because I am ugly and clumsy," rather than, "People in this office are so focused on themselves and their work, no wonder it is so difficult to make conversation with them." A person whose thought patterns exhibit stability believes her unhappiness is permanent. She might think, "I will never succeed." A person whose thought patterns express a lack of control of her situation might believe, "I am miserable because I am clumsy and I cannot change this."

The loss of a loved one can sometimes be a trigger for depression.

The theory of insecure attachments focuses on problems with close relationships as a cause of depression. The loss of a loved one, a history of abandonment, separation, or divorce may increase the chances of a person having depression. Alternatively, depression itself may place strain on relationships and ultimately cause them to end.

Physical changes in the body may also make a person more vulnerable to developing depression. Cancer, a stroke, hormonal disorders, and **Parkinson's disease** are all examples of physical conditions that can lead to depression in which the person experiences feelings of **apathy** and cannot care for himself. The depression can cause him to take longer to recover from his original illness.

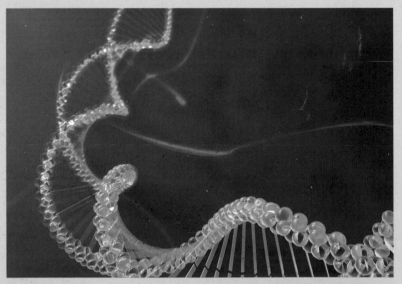

Depression is not caused by DNA alone. Current research shows that depression is caused by the interaction of genetic make-up, personality, and environment.

The vulnerability–stress explanation for the cause of depression incorporates several of the factors discussed, such as genetic influences, thinking habits, and stressful experiences. The general rule of thumb in thinking about the causes of depression is not to oversimplify: current research emphasizes that depression is the result of the interaction of a number of factors specific to each person's biology, personality, and life experiences.

Traumatic events, emotional disturbances, and physical injury can impact brain chemistry in much the same way as biological or chemical influences. In any of these cases, brain chemistry can be changed or become imbalanced enough to cause depression. Depression often results from the brain producing too much or too little of certain chemicals it needs to function normally.

Brain Structure and Communication

Imagine that your brain is a giant communications center, the hub of all your body's communication needs. In order for your body to function, the brain must communicate with itself and with every other part of your body. According to research physicians who have studied this three-pound communications center, the brain sends and receives **billions** of messages in a single day. It uses a complex network of nerve cells called neurons.

Neurons are made up of three structures: dendrites (several branch-like limbs protruding from the cell body, which receive information), the cell body (the neuron's central part, which examines information), and an axon (a single cable-like tail, which sends information). The end of the axon contains several terminal buttons, which overlap the dendrites of other neurons. The neurons, however, don't actually touch each other; they leave a space between called the synapse.

Communication Between Brain Cells: A Bit Like Baseball

Because neurons, the brain's nerve cells, don't actually touch each other, they must use special chemicals called neurotransmitters to send and receive messages. This sending and receiving can be a complicated process.

Imagine that you're an outfielder in a baseball game and you want to send a message to the catcher. You attach a note to the ball in your hand, wind up, swing your arm, release the ball, and throw it toward home plate. The baseball, with message attached, flies through air, across midfield, right into the catcher's glove. Though your center fielder's glove never touched the catcher's glove, you were able to get the message to him. How? You used the ball.

Neurons work together in a similar way in the brain. Using our baseball analogy, you, the center fielder, would be the sending nerve cell, called the presynaptic neuron. The message you want to send is the note attached to the baseball. The catcher would be the receiving cell, called the postsynaptic neuron. To get the message from you, the center fielder (presynaptic neuron), to the catcher (postsynaptic neuron), you have to throw the ball. In the brain, instead of using a baseball to carry the message, the presynaptic neuron (the sending nerve cell) sends its message using chemical neurotransmitters. To throw the ball, the neuron "fires," releasing the neurotransmitters (the baseball) into the synapse (the space between the nerve cells or the space between center field and home) to carry its message.

Once released into the synapse, the neurotransmitter (the ball) looks for the postsynaptic neuron's (receiving cell's or catcher's) receptors (catcher's glove). When the presynaptic neuron's neurotransmitters bind with the postsynaptic neuron's receptors (when the ball finds its way to the glove), the message is delivered.

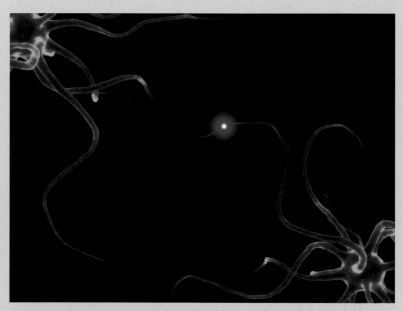

Nerve cells communicate with each other, and send messages to the body, using neurotransmitters. Neurotransmitters, tiny chemical packets of information, are fired across a synapse to be collected by the next nerve cell and so on down the line.

Once the message is delivered (when the catcher takes your note off the ball), the receiving cell (the catcher) doesn't need the neurotransmitter anymore (the ball), so it releases the neurotransmitters back into the synapse (throws the ball, without its message, back into the air between home and center field). These used neurotransmitters will remain in the synapse (the ball will stay between the home and the center field) until the original sending cell (the center fielder) takes them back (center fielder catches or picks up the ball). This process of taking neurotransmitters back again is called reuptake.

Now imagine that you want to send a billion messages to the catcher. You'd need quite a few baseballs to send those messages! Scientists estimate the brain uses more than a million neurons to send messages over a quadrillion synapses.

Problems in Brain Communication

Though it sounds easy, communication in the brain is a complicated process made up of several steps, any of which can run into problems:

- The presynaptic neuron doesn't fire correctly (center fielder has a poor arm).

- The brain doesn't produce enough neurotransmitters (there aren't enough balls to carry the messages).

- The postsynaptic neuron has too few receptors (catcher doesn't catch well or doesn't have a glove).

- The postsynaptic neuron's receptors get blocked (a base runner blocks the catcher's glove, keeping the catcher from catching the ball).

- Enzymes (other brain chemicals) destroy too much of the neurotransmitters remaining in the synapse (fans steal the balls before they're caught).

- Too much or too little neurotransmitter is taken back by the sending cell (the center fielder hogs the used ball or drops the ball when it's returned).

Any disruption of the communication process between neurons can result in psychological disorders.

Depression results primarily from problems with neurotransmitters: how they are released, how much neurotransmitter is present, how much is taken back by the sending cell. To date, scientists have identified over twenty kinds of neurotransmitters in the brain, with each being used in multiple parts of the brain. They have also found links between certain neurotransmitters and specific psychological conditions. Depression and bipolar disorder are both linked to the neurotransmitters serotonin, **norepinephrine**, and **dopamine**.

Chapter 4
Hope

ould Dr. Graham really help her—or was Ashley getting her hopes up for nothing? Ashley had plenty of time to sit and think while driving in the slow-moving traffic, looking at the back of the van in front of her. In her mind, Ashley saw herself the week before, sitting on the living room couch, earnestly pleading with her father, who sat opposite her on a wicker chair, his expression blank.

"Dad, listen, there's a lot going on in my life and I could really use some help."

"That's why we went to see the doctor, and he prescribed medicine for you."

"I appreciate that, Dad, really. But it isn't working; my life just keeps getting worse. I hate getting up every day, I'm failing at everything."

Her father sat still, impossible to read, but his silence encouraged Ashley to press her case.

"I have a friend at school, Josh—and I know his sister, Andrea. Josh says Andrea had depression like I have now, and this psychiatrist, Dr. Graham, really helped her. Dad, please, I want to see this therapist."

Her father shook his head. "We don't have much extra money, and I'd hate to spend it on a wild-goose chase."

"Dad, please, at least let me see her a few times, and then we can decide if she's worth it."

"Well." Her father looked at her for a long time. Ashley squirmed in her seat, unable to tell what he was thinking. "I guess that can't hurt," he said finally. "Just for a few months."

It was a grudging permission, but Ashley was thankful nonetheless.

She was jarred back to the present moment as traffic stopped suddenly. She slammed on the brakes, stopping just inches from the minivan in front of her. Drivers all around her were beeping their horns, expressing frustration with the unexpected stop, with the traffic jam, with life in general.

What would Dr. Graham be like? Ashley didn't know much about psychiatrists. Her impressions were mostly formed from old movies, where therapists were men who talked with German accents and wore long white beards, round glasses, and stuffy suits. She wondered if Dr. Graham would be a female version of Dr. Freud: "Yah, zee problem ees you ver not potty trained in zee right way—vee have to regress now to der childhood."

Finally, she pulled her little car into the parking garage and found an open space on the third floor. From there, she took the elevator to the main floor of the building. She sat for a few minutes in the receptionist's office where she filled out a form, then found a *Rolling Stone* among the pile of magazines; she glanced through an article while waiting nervously until the receptionist told her, "Ashley Gordon, you can go in now."

Ashley sucked in a deep breath and stepped through the door. A surprisingly young woman, dressed as cool as anyone she knew, greeted her and then ushered Ashley into a comfortable stuffed chair.

Ashley looked around the office. "What, no couch?"

Dr. Graham chuckled, "No—today's teens are too sleep-deprived. Can't have you falling asleep on me, that would be a real waste of your time, wouldn't it?"

At least she has a sense of humor, Ashley thought to herself.

"Ashley, it says on your form that you've been struggling with depression lately?"

"I guess so, that's what everyone tells me. I just feel like crap all the time, sad and tired out and hopeless."

"And how long have you felt this way?"

"That's hard to say. It's been at least six months. I think more maybe."

Dr. Graham nodded again. "Ashley, I want to tell you what you can expect from me. I practice what we call cognitive behavioral therapy. That means we'll be talking a lot about your relationships and how you think about things. Frankly, effective therapy isn't always easy. I promise I'll never ask you anything intended to humiliate or hurt you, but sometimes we all have to face things about ourselves that are difficult. The good news is this: cognitive therapy is at least as effective as antidepressant medications, and when combined with medicine and other practices, it is more effective yet. So we'll also be looking at the medications that may help you to get well faster."

Ashley was surprised at Dr. Graham's frankness, but she appreciated the way the therapist was treating her like an adult. "That's fine, Dr. Graham. I can't imagine anything I might discover about myself being more difficult than what I'm already living through."

Dr. Graham proceeded to ask questions about Ashley's childhood, her home, school, and her ideas about life in general. She appeared interested in all Ashley's answers, so

Ashley shared more and more openly. Before she knew it, their hour together was up.

Dr. Graham got to her feet, signaling that their time together was over. "Ashley, I'm looking forward to working with you. You're very thoughtful and articulate, and that will help you a lot in treating your depression."

For the first time that day, Ashley flashed a brief smile.

"Next week we can talk more directly about your depression, but there's something I'd like you to do in the meantime."

"What's that?"

"I'd like you to keep a daily diary—one you'll be sharing with me, so don't write down anything you don't want me to know. At the end of each day, list the things that you think were important that day and how you feel about them. Bring it with you next week, okay?"

"All right, I can do that."

Dr. Graham handed her a neatly printed piece of paper. "Here's a card with an emergency number you can call if you ever need someone to talk to in a pinch."

Ashley nodded.

"Shall we meet the same time next week, then?"

"Yeah, that's good."

"Great! I'll see you then." Dr. Graham shook hands with Ashley and walked with her to the door.

Outside the building, Ashley paused for a minute, looking at the busy street, squinting in the bright sun, and breathing in the cool coastal air. She waited for the familiar rush of panic to hit her, but for once it didn't come. *Wow!* she thought. *Pretty cool.*

The following week passed without any major incidents, and before she knew it, it was time once again for Ashley to visit Dr. Graham's office. As promised, Ashley read her diary for the therapist. As she did so, Dr. Graham would gently interrupt and ask questions. Toward the end of their session, Dr. Graham made several suggestions.

"I'd like to continue meeting every week for at least several months," she concluded. "As I said before, we'll talk about your relationships and feelings, and I'll be making suggestions for those each week."

"That would be fine. In fact . . . I'd like that."

"Good! But talking is only part of the treatment. I think it's important for you to go back on your medication."

Ashley's face fell. "I hate taking them. They scare me."

Dr. Graham looked thoughtful. "How would you feel about trying a nonprescription herbal supplement?"

Ashley was surprised a psychiatrist would suggest an herbal remedy.

"Hypericum—what's more commonly called St. John's wort—might be a good choice for you. Do you think you would feel more comfortable with that?"

"Maybe. I wouldn't be as nervous about it as I am about the other medicine I was taking."

"Prescription antidepressants are actually quite safe and effective, but a person's beliefs about a medicine can make a big difference in how it affects them. For now, keep taking the medicine your other doctor prescribed. You'll need to come off it gradually."

Ashley flashed a smile at Dr. Graham, brief but genuine. Finally, someone was listening to her, respecting her feelings.

"And Ashley, there's one more thing I want you to do for your treatment."

"Yes?"

"Depression is a very complex disease; it attacks your thinking, your feelings, and your body—all at the same time. That's why it is so painful, and so hard to treat. That's also why it requires a holistic approach to get feeling better."

Ashley struggled to absorb all the new information. "A holistic approach?"

"Yes, treating your thinking, your emotions, and your physical health at the same time. Our conversations can help with the thinking part, we'll continue to address chemical ways to work with your emotions, but you also need to take part in some sort of physical exercise on a regular basis."

"Yes, but I feel so tired all the time. I can't imagine dragging myself down to the health club every week."

"It will be easier if you do something you naturally enjoy. Like . . . why don't you haul out your board and some wax and head for the shore?"

"But. . ." Ashley struggled to put her reluctance into words. "There's this heaviness all through my body. Like I can barely make myself move. I don't even know if I could make it out to the line-up."

"Ashley, no one's expecting you to get out there and surf like a world champion. The point is—you need exercise to get feeling better, and it'll be easier to do something you're already good at."

Ashley sighed. "Okay."

"Good. See you next week, then?"

"See you next week."

They shook hands, and Ashley left, still trying to absorb everything Dr. Graham had said. *Go to weekly therapy, keep taking medication, and exercise on top of coping with school and home? That's a lot to do when I feel like life is already unbearable.*

Though Ashley was inclined to trust Dr. Graham, it was hard to shake the helpless feelings that had become such a familiar part of her everyday life. She had an awful foreboding that disaster was lurking just around the corner.

How Are Depression and Anxiety Treated?

When a teen's emotions become overwhelming to the point that they're interfering with her ability to carry out the responsibilities of her normal life—or even if they're to the point that they merely seem an enormous load to carry—she should talk about what she's experiencing with an adult she trusts. Going on to seek psychological help is one option she should be sure to bring up. A good place to start is the family doctor. Oftentimes, he may decide that short-term use of a psychiatric medication may help the teen regain control of her emotions.

Antidepressants

An antidepressant is a drug used to treat depression. Most antidepressants fall into three main categories based on the chemical structure of the drugs and how they work in the human body:

- monoamine oxidase inhibitors (MAOIs)
- selective serotonin reuptake inhibitors (SSRIs)
- tricyclic antidepressants

Much of the current research on antidepressants has been founded on a hypothesis developed in the 1960s called the catecholamine hypothesis. According to this hypothesis, the main biological cause of depression is a chemical imbalance in the brain. When certain brain chemicals responsible for maintaining stable moods and emotions become depleted, depression seems to follow. To counteract the depletion of these important chemicals, an

A doctor may prescribe antidepressants or antianxiety medications to help a teen regain control of his emotions.

effective antidepressant drug should increase the amounts of these chemicals in the brain, helping to restore them to usual levels. The three types of antidepressants listed above work based on this principle, but scientists still do not know exactly how each antidepressant behaves in the brain to alleviate the symptoms of depression.

Antianxiety Medications

Psychiatric drugs are also one of the most common methods for treating serious anxiety disorders. Some of the same drugs used to treat depression also help with anxiety, but there are other drugs as well that are particularly targeted at reducing anxiety. Medication may be a short-term therapy, or it may be required for a lengthy period of time, depending on the individual.

The SSRI Paxil® (paroxetine) has been approved for social anxiety disorder (social phobia), GAD, and panic disorder; Zoloft® (sertraline) is approved for panic disorder; and Effexor® (venlafaxine) has been approved for GAD.

Medications specifically designed to treat anxiety include the benzodiazepines, which can relieve symptoms within a short time. Benzodiazepines vary in duration of action in different people; they may be taken two or three times a day, sometimes only once a day, or just on an "as-needed" basis. Dosage is generally started at a low level and gradually increased until symptoms are diminished or removed. The dosage will vary a great deal depending on the symptoms and the individual's body chemistry. Commonly used benzodiazepines include Klonopin® (clonazepam), Xanax® (alprazolam), Valium® (diazepam), and Ativan® (lorazepam).

The only medication other than the benzodiazepines specifically for treating anxiety disorders is BuSpar® (buspirone). Unlike the benzodiazepines, buspirone must be taken consistently for at least two weeks to achieve an antianxiety effect and therefore cannot be used on an as-needed basis.

Beta-blockers, medications often used to treat heart conditions and high blood pressure, are sometimes used to control "performance anxiety" when the individual must face a specific stressful situation—a speech, a presentation in class, or an important meeting. Propranolol (Inderal®, Inderide®) is a commonly used beta-blocker for this type of short-term anxiety, but it should only be taken when anxiety is overwhelming.

~~~~~~

The Risks of Medication

A side effect is an unwanted result that goes hand-in-hand with the main effect. One of aspirin's main effects, for instance, is to relieve pain. However, aspirin often causes stomach bleeding. In relieving pain, the aspirin might also upset your stomach. An upset stomach, then, is a side effect of aspirin. It's not wanted, but it goes along with relieving pain.

Antidepressants' Side Effects

Antidepressants can cause the following undesired effects:

- dry mouth
- urinary retention
- blurred vision
- constipation
- sedation (can interfere with driving or operating machinery)
- sleep disruption
- weight gain
- headache
- nausea
- gastrointestinal disturbance/diarrhea
- abdominal pain
- sexual difficulties
- agitation
- anxiety

Some critics of SSRIs claim that these drugs can cause both suicidal and homicidal behavior, especially when they are given to young adults. Although these risks are still not clear, in 2004, the U.S. Food and Drug Administration ordered that Zoloft and similar antidepressants carry warnings that they "increase the risk of suicidal thinking and behavior" in children with depression and other psychiatric disorders. These drugs also carry a warning for adults, noting that antidepressants can cause anxiety, irritability, hostility, aggressiveness, and impulsiveness.

People taking MAOIs must be careful of their diet while they are on the medication. Cheese, chicken livers, broad-bean pods, and other foods cause an amine called tyramine to rush to the brain. Tyramine affects blood pressure, and under normal conditions, monoamines handle this influx. But, if someone is on MAOIs, monoamines cannot do their job, and this tyramine build up can cause a spike in blood pressure, sometimes leading to a stroke.

Medications can help get emotions under control, but treatment of a mood disorder should also include counseling from a trained professional.

Side Effects of Antianxiety Medications

Benzodiazepines have relatively few side effects: drowsiness and loss of coordination are most common; fatigue and mental slowing or confusion can also occur. These effects make it dangerous for people taking benzodiazepines to drive or operate some machinery. Other side effects are rare. However, it is wise to abstain from alcohol when taking benzodiazepines, because the interaction between benzodiazepines and alcohol can lead to serious and possibly life-threatening complications. It is also important to tell the doctor about other medications you might be taking. People taking benzodiazepines for weeks or months may develop tolerance for and dependence on these drugs. Abuse and withdrawal reactions are also possible. For these reasons, the medications are generally prescribed for only brief periods of time—days or weeks—and sometimes just for stressful situations or anxiety attacks. However, some patients may need long-term treatment.

Never stop taking a benzodiazepine without talking to your doctor. A withdrawal reaction may occur if the treatment is stopped abruptly. Symptoms may include anxiety, shakiness, headache, dizziness, sleeplessness, loss of appetite, or in extreme cases, **seizures**. A withdrawal reaction may be mistaken for a return of the anxiety because many of the symptoms are similar. After a person has taken benzodiazepines for an extended period, the dosage is gradually reduced before it is stopped completely.

Other antianxiety medications, like BuSpar, do not have as many side effects as benzodiazepines do. The most commonly noted side effects associated with these medications are nausea, headache, nervousness, lightheadedness, excitement, and insomnia.

Who Is Qualified to Provide Psychological Treatment?

If you or someone you know decides to seek treatment for overwhelming emotions, be aware that there is wide variety of professionals who work in this field. These include:

- psychiatrists: medical doctors who specialize in treating mental and emotional problems. They can prescribe medication as treatment for depression and anxiety.

- psychologists: mental health professionals, often holding a Ph.D or other graduate degree in psychology, who have extensive training in mental health issues, counseling skills, testing and evaluation methods, and treatment strategies. Though highly trained, psychologists are not medical doctors and cannot prescribe medication.

- psychiatric nurse practitioners: specially trained nurses who provide care in large health care organizations and in the community. They function independently and collaboratively with other health-care team members to provide comprehensive treatment that will increase the probability of a successful outcome.

- therapists: mental health workers who may (or may not) be trained in certain types of psychotherapeutic methods. They may or may not hold counseling degrees and are often unregulated. They cannot prescribe any form of medication.

- licensed therapists: trained mental health workers who are under the supervision of and accountable to a licensing board (state, federal, organizational, etc.). They cannot prescribe medications.

- counselors: these professionals are trained to give more generalized advice about life issues. They may or may not hold counseling degrees, but they cannot prescribe medications.

- pastoral counselors: ministers, pastors, priests, or rabbis who are trained in counseling methods or psychotherapy skills. Their counsel will include matters of faith.

Supportive Therapies

Psychiatric drugs are not magic pills that will automatically make a teen's life wonderful. Even though they can often offer real help, there will still be issues the teen will need to address. Most professionals believe that supportive therapies are a vital part of any treatment plan.

These are what we often think of as "counseling," and they focus on providing support for a patient by providing counseling relationships where the patient can be listened to and reassured. It is a form of mental health help that involves talking with a psychiatrist, psychologist, therapist, or counselor to work through problems, resolve conflicts, and learn effective ways of coping with stress or difficult emotions. Professionals in supportive therapies often listen to a patient's current problems and suggest ways to handle them. These relationships can be short term or long term.

When a person seeks counseling, the specific kind of help she receives may vary, depending on the therapist's beliefs. The differences between psychotherapies are their goals and how long it takes to achieve them.

Cognitive Therapy

This is a type of psychotherapy that tries to help patients replace negative thoughts with positive ones. It focuses on helping someone with a mood disorder learn how to *think* differently. It teaches patients how to tell themselves good things in their minds. Instead of thinking, *I never do anything right*, the patient might tell himself to think: **Well, you might not have done the best job on this one thing, but look at all the other things you do well.** Patients can usually respond to this kind of therapy in a fairly short time.

Behavioral Therapy

This form of therapy focuses on helping patients change the way they *behave*. It equips the patient to act in ways that will make her feel more fulfilled and satisfied, and to help her *unlearn* old patterns or habits that make her feel worse. Results from behavioral therapy can be both short term and long term.

Interpersonal Therapy

This helps the patient improve relationship and communication skills, resolve conflict, grow in people skills, and deal with unresolved grief. The focus is primarily on how to get along with others in healthy ways. This type of help requires several months of therapy.

Psychodynamic Therapy

A professional who uses this approach examines past issues and experiences that influence how the patient thinks, feels, and acts today. She will tend to focus less on "how-to" skills and more on thoughts and feelings, and the therapy usually lasts longer than other forms of treatment do. Some patients take years to respond to psychodynamic therapy.

Most health professionals today are trained in one or more of these therapies (there are others). But not all mental health workers use all types of therapy. Some use one type of therapy, while others use several at the same or alternating times. Some will start a patient on one kind of therapy, then switch to another. Some treat patients one-on-one; others work with patients in groups. Treatment styles and methods vary.

Alternatives to Medication

If your moods feel overwhelming, there are also other things you can do that may help you regain control of your emotions.

Exercise

Though doctors commonly tell patients on mood disorder drugs to try psychotherapy, it is not the only supplementary treatment available. Doctors almost always recommend exercise, too, because of how exercise impacts the chemicals (especially neurotransmitters) in the brain.

In a study done at Duke University, 156 adults with mild to moderate major depression were given one of three treatment options:

1. exercise for forty-five minutes three times a week, but don't take medication;

2. take an antidepressant, but don't exercise;

3. do both (exercise forty-five minutes three times a week *and* take an antidepressant).

After four months, the people who *only exercised* experienced as much improvement in their depression as the people who only took medication or who did both. After an additional six months, researchers observed that the people who continued to exercise regularly were the least likely to have their depressions come back again.

Exercise provides health benefits. It gives us added energy, better sleep, a healthier heart and lungs, improved self-esteem, and reduced irritability. Anxiety and depression can cause low energy, sleep problems, low self-esteem, and increased anger, so exercise seems like the perfect **antidote** for a person who struggles with one!

As always, it's important to talk to your doctor before you start an exercise program. If she says to go ahead, start slowly. Pick an exercise you enjoy that works easily into your daily schedule. Shoot for thirty minutes of continuous (not start-and-stop) exercise at least four days a week.

Chapter 5
Into the Abyss

shley would never have guessed that an invitation at lunch could lead to the worst night of her life. She was mildly surprised on Friday when Paige Sun sat down beside her at the Marina High cafeteria. Paige was part of the crowd that Stacie and Ashley used to hang out with, but Ashley had withdrawn from Paige along with the others. But now here was Paige, so Ashley tried to pull herself out of her shell and be social. They exchanged typical high school gossip and Paige said, "Hey, there's a party tonight at Joe Braxton's house. I don't want to go alone—you want to come with me? I could pick you up."

"Joe Braxton's place? Didn't he trash his parents' house with a party last year?"

"Yeah. I hear they had to pay a thousand dollars to repair the damage."

"And he's doing it again?"

"Yep. The dude's crazy. His parents are spending the week at a condo in Hawaii, so—it's party time!"

Ashley wasn't a big fan of the party scene, but she had been feeling better after six weeks of visiting Dr. Graham. The psychiatrist had suggested Ashley push herself a bit to be more social, so she agreed to go.

That night it seemed every kid in Huntington Beach was at Joe's house. Cars were parked up and down the street, and kids streamed in and out of the spacious two-story residence. In the backyard, music pumped from an enormous pair of speakers. DJ Zap, popular at Marina High parties, was manning the deck. Several kegs of beer stood in the kitchen, and bottles of vodka and wine coolers lined the countertop. With all the commotion and noise, Ashley wondered how long before someone on the street would call the cops with a complaint—but in the meantime, it would be some wild party.

Ashley and Paige sat in a backyard gazebo with a circle of kids. The boys bragged about their real or imagined sexual and surfing exploits, and the girls kept up a lively jabber poking fun at the guys' testosterone-laden remarks. All the while, a bong circulated around the gazebo.

Ashley was by no means a pothead, but she smoked socially on occasion, so she took the plastic cylinder when it was handed to her and sucked in a deep breath of the cool, sweet-smelling smoke. The bong went round the gazebo again, laughter and trash talk filling the night air. After taking her second hit, Ashley had a sudden realization: *I feel good tonight!* She was astounded; how long had it been since she felt happy about anything? For months, Ashley had thought of her life as varying degrees of unhappiness, subtly blending shades of black and gray. But tonight, after a couple of hits on that bong, she actually felt at peace.

Her confidence renewed, Ashley decided to circulate around the party. She said hello to people she had not spoken to in months; said, "How are you?" and "Where have you been?" to students she hardly knew. The music was playing even louder than before, the bass beats pushing on her chest and tingling the soles of her feet. DJ Zap was playing a remix of the Pussycat Dolls, looping the chorus over and over, "Don't cha wish your girlfriend was hot like me?" and everyone in the yard seemed to be moving to the rhythm. Ashley began dancing; her feet barely seemed to touch the ground.

After what seemed a happy eternity, Ashley stumbled back to the gazebo, took another hit off the bong, and emptied a wine cooler. Things were getting blurry . . . she felt happy, woozy.

The next thing Ashley knew, something felt funny on her chest. She opened her eyes, tried to focus: there was a hand pushing up her blouse. *What?* She screamed and slapped, saw the boy next to her recoil with a surprised look on his face.

Ashley jumped to her feet and then reeled with dizziness; she felt suddenly nauseated. She grabbed her mouth with both hands and staggered from the gazebo to the bushes, where she puked harder than she remembered ever puking before. Then she tried to walk back toward the house, but her legs didn't feel like they were attached to her torso. Everything was spinning, fading in and out of focus.

The night's happy feelings had gone completely; she was now consumed by utter panic. She couldn't believe a stranger was feeling her up . . . couldn't believe she had let herself get so wasted. She hated herself, hated the boy, hated Paige for bringing her, and hated this party. *Get out of here!* her mind screamed.

She headed for the house, reached the back porch entrance, and *bam!* She smashed into the glass of the sliding door. She shoved it aside and walked through. There was something on her white T-shirt . . . red spots appearing

. . . weird. She brushed her nose with her hand and saw more red, like watercolor paint. *Oh no*, she realized, *I have a bloody nose.* She heard laughter and looked toward the side of the room, where Vanna Khan was staring at her and chuckling.

Ashley staggered through the living room and plowed out through the front door onto the lawn. Her legs gave way, and she collapsed in a heap. She was trembling, her heart beating like she thought it would burst. "Hey, somebody!" she yelled, "Someone take me home. I have to get home. Now!"

Ashley was unaware of the ride home. Her next memory was lying in her own front yard, crawling toward the front porch. She reached up for the door knob, turned it. . . . It was locked. She reached for her purse, but it wasn't on her shoulder: she had left it behind at the party. She felt acid burning up the back of her throat again, so she turned her head quickly into the bush next to her and puked. As she vomited pink fluid into the bush, she was dimly aware that the door had opened.

She turned her head. Her father was looking down at her.

"Ashley! What is going on?"

Her head spinning, Ashley couldn't have answered if she wanted.

"Look at you! I can't believe it. Look at your clothes, all covered with filth. You don't even look like my daughter!"

With enormous effort, Ashley staggered to her feet and stumbled past her father, into the house, and toward the stairs. Her legs failed, but she grasped the railing and pulled herself up the steps.

"Where were you? Did you do drugs? Did you? Answer me!"

Ashley didn't even look behind her. She crawled into her room, slammed the door with her foot, and collapsed onto her bed. She felt worse than she could ever remember.

How could she ever walk into Marina High again? Everyone at school would remember Ashley drunk, Ashley passed out in the gazebo while some boy tried to take advantage of her, Ashley puking and banging into the glass and yelling like a nut on the front lawn. She had been trying so hard to be positive and overcome her depression—now she had messed up everything. Her father was sure to make her life a living hell; he wouldn't let her forget this night.

Ashley felt despair like black waves pushing her down and drowning her. What could she do? Then she remembered the card Dr. Graham had given her; it was on the nightstand beside her bed. Ashley's fingers moved clumsily, as though they were connected to her hand only with loose strings, but she managed to pull her cell phone out of her pants pocket and dial the number.

She was answered by a message: "Dr. Monica Graham is not available. Please wait while we redirect your call to Redondo Hospital Emergency Center." Ashley didn't want to talk to some stranger. No stranger could help her on a night like this. She pushed the "off" button.

She lay on her bed, sobbing quietly into the soft mattress. Panic and despair were suffocating her. What could she do?

Then, suddenly, she knew the answer. It came to her clearly, like a shaft of light piercing the darkness. She didn't have to go through these awful feelings; she could be free.

Ashley waited on her bed until she knew she could walk steadily. Then she quietly crept out of her room and down the hall to the upstairs bathroom. She turned on the light and opened the closet. There, she found some of her mother's old prescriptions: sleeping pills, tranquilizers. She stuffed the pills into her mouth, a whole handful, and washed them all down with a glass of water. Calm now, she went back to her room.

In a few minutes, she felt her body numbing. The panic and gloom gave way to a pleasant sensation, one where nothing mattered. She whispered, "I'm coming Stacie. I'm going to be free soon, just like you are." Her heart beat slower and slower. Then . . .

What Causes Anxiety?

At one time, anxiety was viewed as a signal of a person's defenses against uncomfortable memories and feelings. This theory was based on the pioneering work of Sigmund Freud (1856–1939), the Austrian founder of **psychoanalysis**. According to this system

Sigmund Freud, the founder of psychoanalysis, viewed anxiety as an individual's defense against uncomfortable memories and feelings.

The fight-or-flight response evolved in humans as a reaction to dangerous situations. If an early human encountered a lion while hunting, he had to decide quickly to either fight or run away.

of thought, anxiety was really a signal of deeper emotional conflict.

Since then, other theories have been developed to explain human emotions, and each of them look at anxiety a little differently. Psychodynamic theory recognizes other factors, including problems in interpersonal relationships, that may be involved in the development of anxiety disorders. Behaviorists attribute anxiety disorders to **maladaptive** learning based on conditioned emotional responses. The chemical imbalance theory of anxiety disorders comes from the biological model of the mind, a way of looking at the mind that suggests psychiatric disorders, including both anxiety and depression, result from abnormalities in the brain's biological makeup.

In general, though, we can understand anxiety better if we think about how our bodies react to fear. The body's reaction to fear is called the fight or flight response. People have had it since the beginning of time. When early human beings faced a wild animal, they had two choices: try to overcome the animal (fight) or run away (flight). Our bodies are still made to respond with the same two choices in the face of any perceived danger. But in our modern-day world, fight or flight doesn't work for every danger we face.

But our bodies don't know that, and they're busy getting ready for either quick action or quick escape. Heart rate increases in order to pump more blood to the muscles and brain; lungs work faster to supply the body with more oxygen; the pupils get larger to enable optimum vision; and the digestive and urinary systems slow down temporarily so all the body's energy can go toward dealing with the crisis.

All these physical reactions are fine, so long as you're going to be expending actual physical energy. But when your mind tells your body that there's some sort of danger—say a big test that's coming up, or your parents fighting, or troubles with a romantic relationship—and there's nothing your body can do to help, then those physical responses to danger can make you feel physically unwell. You might have tightness in your chest or a stomachache, you might feel dizzy or jumpy, and you may have trouble relaxing enough to fall asleep at night. These feelings are called anxiety, and when they go on and on without letting up, they can interfere with daily life.

How Is Depression Diagnosed?

If a person is depressed, she feels sad day after day, and the smallest things may make her cry. Life looks bleak and hopeless, and she may forget what it was like not to be sad. Life may seem gray and boring; she may have little or no desire to do her homework or other responsibilities; she may not want to read, watch television, or do any of the things she would normally enjoy; and she may prefer to be alone all the time, rather than with her friends and family. Chances are, she'll start believing that she will never feel right again. In worst-case scenarios, she may begin to think about suicide.

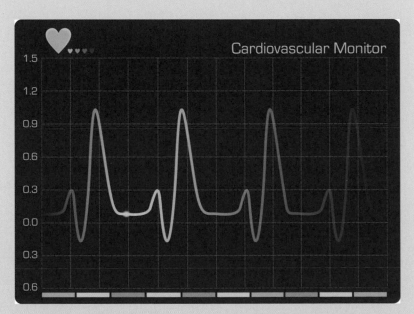

During the fight or flight response, a person's heart rate increases in order to pump more blood to the muscles and brain. This gives her more strength and speed and allows her to think more clearly.

According to the DSM-IV, a person has major depressive disorder if he has experienced at least five of the following symptoms for at least two weeks:

- He feels depressed, sad, blue, tearful.

- He has lost interest or pleasure in things he previously liked to do.

- His appetite is much less or much greater than usual and he has lost or gained weight.

- He has trouble sleeping or sleeps too much.

- He is so agitated, restless, or slowed down that others have begun to notice.

- He is tired and has no energy.

- He feels worthless or excessively guilty about things he has done or not done.

- He has trouble concentrating, thinking clearly, or making decisions.

- He feels he would be better off dead or has thoughts about killing himself.

These symptoms need to be severe enough to upset the person's daily routine, or to seriously impair his work, or to interfere with his relationships. The depression cannot have a specific cause like alcohol, drugs, medication side effects, or physical illness, and it cannot be just a normal reaction to the death of a loved one.

Studies show that 74 percent of people seeking help for depression go to their primary care physician, and that 50 percent of these cases are misdiagnosed. Some of these misdiagnoses may occur because the

If an individual is depressed, she will feel down day after day. She might feel overwhelmed by or cry over seemingly insignificant things.

patients are treated for physical symptoms such as sleep problems, fatigue, or weight loss, without considering depression as a possible root cause. When diagnosing for depression, tests should be given to rule out any *organic* factors—such as nutrient deficiencies, **hypothyroidism**, or reactions to drugs—that can produce similar symptoms.

How Is Anxiety Diagnosed?

Effective treatment for anxiety, like depression, always starts with a correct diagnosis, so a doctor will first rule out possible biological causes for anxiety.

Rare medical conditions that can cause anxiety-like symptoms include thyroid disorders, **hypoglycemia**, **Cushing's disease**, and pheochromocytoma (a tumor of the adrenal gland). Medications such as theophylline preparations for asthma and decongestants such as pseudoephedrine and phenylephrine can also cause anxiety. Caffeine, which is found in coffee, tea, soda, and chocolate, frequently makes anxiety worse. Although alcohol and nicotine (in tobacco) may initially relax users, both substances increase anxiety in the long run.

Although anxiety disorders are so common among teens and children, it is often not recognized, and most who have an anxiety disorder do not receive treatment. Common signs of anxiety in young people include excessive worrying about ordinary activities, such as going to school or summer camp, taking a test, or performing in sports. At times, the emotional sensations will be accompanied by physical symptoms such as palpitations, sweating, trembling, stomachache, or headache. The young person may avoid certain situations he perceives to be the sources of his anxiety (such as school or social situations). This avoidance can cause social withdrawal. When these symptoms cause extreme distress and interfere with the young person's functioning in everyday activities, he is diagnosed as having an anxiety disorder.

What Should I Do If My Emotions Feel Overwhelming?

- First, depression and anxiety in teens are not conditions you will automatically outgrow.

Pay attention to your feelings. Take your emotions seriously and don't dismiss them.

• Second, dark thoughts of death and suicide should always be taken seriously. The National Mental Heath Association notes that nearly all people who attempt suicide speak about it (and think about it) first.

• Third, getting help for depression and anxiety requires more than just popping a pill. Learning how to communicate with family members, how to reduce stress, how to cope with and manage feelings—these are all parts of the recovery process. Counseling and therapy, in addition to medication, are often necessary to help a person with a mood disorder get well.

• Fourth, if you are depressed or struggling with anxiety, you can't beat it on your own. The good news is that help is available today that can effectively treat your symptoms and get you back on the road of normal life. You just need to be willing to ask for and receive the help you need.

Chapter 6
On Waking

shley, thank goodness you're all right!"

"Dr. Graham, what are you doing here?"

Ashley sat up in her hospital bed, and Dr. Graham grasped her hands, then sat down in a chair beside the bed.

"Your father called me. He told me about the drug overdose and how he called emergency services when he found you. Thank heavens they got you here in time."

"Yeah, well, I suppose he did me a favor."

Dr. Graham looked troubled. "Can you tell me why you took those pills?"

Ashley recounted the disgusting events of the previous night. After she finished, Dr. Graham said, "No wonder you felt so awful. All those different substances were a nasty mixture."

"What do you mean?"

"It wasn't just the marijuana and the drinks that affected you last night; you have a good dose of St. John's wort and some of the remaining prescription medication in your body as well. They all combined to overwhelm your nervous system."

"But I felt so good for a while. After a few hits of grass and a couple of drinks, I felt happier than I have for a long time."

Dr. Graham nodded. "Yes, that's why many teens with depression also take illegal drugs. At first it feels as if you've found a better treatment than the legal ones—but in the end you're left worse off than before."

Ashley agreed, "That's what happened all right."

"What now?" Dr. Graham asked.

Ashley felt anxiety gripping her ribcage. She closed her eyes and took a deep breath. "I don't know how I'm going to face the next few days," she confessed. "Everyone at school is going to know about the party. I can't imagine walking into school and putting up with the stares, the gossip, and all the crap they're going to give me."

Dr. Graham thought for a minute. "Do you think you were the only one behaving foolishly at that party?"

Ashley shook her head. "No, there were others."

"Could it be that the others were too intoxicated to be paying attention to you?"

Ashley agreed that could be the case, but there was something else troubling her. "Why did I do all those stupid things: get stoned, embarrass myself, and try to commit suicide? It seems like I'm just going further downhill."

"Ashley, you are doing well coping with your depression. You are improving, but every stage of life has its perils. Even if your depression and anxiety went away completely, there would still be challenges in life."

Ashley lay back on the bed. "Yeah, like dealing with my dad."

"Yes, that is a challenge. Even if you didn't have the biochemical pull toward depression, you would still have a struggle coping with your father's illness. But there are people who can help you with that. Have you heard of Alateen?"

"What is it, another medicine?"

"No, it's a group for adolescents with alcoholic parents. They'll give you support to help cope with your dad's drinking, and I think that will help you manage your depression as well."

"How do I find them?"

"Just look up the name in the phone book and call the number. There are groups meeting all different times and places around town."

"I guess I can give it a try."

Dr. Graham looked into Ashley's face and was silent for a moment. Then she asked, "Ashley, do you still want to commit suicide?"

Ashley thought for a long moment. "I don't think so. Right now I'm glad to be alive. But just before I drifted off, I thought I was going to be with Stacie again and be free from all the pain I have to put up with every day. Death seemed so inviting."

"How do you know what death would be like?" asked Dr. Graham. "Do you have any guarantees you'd be happier in another life than you are in this one?"

Ashley was taken aback by the question. She wasn't sure how to answer.

Dr. Graham leaned closer. "Ashley, I want to ask you something, and I want you to take this very seriously."

"Yes?"

"Promise me if you ever think of committing suicide again you'll contact me, and you'll do nothing to hurt your-self before we can get together. Do you promise me that?"

"Yes, I promise."

After Dr. Graham left, Ashley lay in her bed, eyes wide open. She thought back over the sadness and anxiety she had felt in the past months and the trials she had endured. She wondered what kind of future lay ahead.

Most teens who attempt suicide say they did it because they were trying to escape from a situation that seemed impossible to deal with or to get relief from really bad thoughts or feelings. They didn't want to die as much as they wanted to escape from what was going on. And at that particular moment, dying seemed like the only way out. But suicide is a permanent solution to a temporary situation. Everything changes, sooner or later, and even the worst situation doesn't last forever.

We all feel overwhelmed by difficult emotions or situations sometimes. But most people get through it or can put their problems in perspective and find a way to carry on with determination and hope. So why does one person try suicide when another person in the same tough situation does not? What makes some people better able to deal with life's setbacks than others? What makes a person unable to see another way out of a bad situation besides ending his or her life?

The answer to those questions lies in the fact that most people who commit suicide have depression. Depression clouds people's perceptions, makes them unable to assess a situation clearly, and makes even small problems seem overwhelming.

Male vs. Female Suicide

Teen girls attempt suicide more often than males—but boys are four times more likely to succeed when they do try to commit suicide. This is because guys are more apt to use more deadly methods—like guns. Over half of all "successful" suicide attempts involve a gun.

More females than males attempt suicide, but more males than females actually commit suicide. This is because a boy is more likely to use a deadly method, such as a gun.

When Is It Time to Get Help?

If you recognize these symptoms in yourself or a loved one seek help:

- frequent sadness, tearfulness, crying, helplessness
- bouts of hostility or rage
- low energy or lack of interest in activities
- overreaction to criticism, rejection, or failure
- low self-esteem or destructive self-criticism
- unusual irritability or anger
- desire to withdraw or be alone, or a pervading sense of isolation

- frequent stomachaches or headaches
- poor concentration or inability to make decisions
- changes in school performance (skipping school, slipping grades)
- sleep trouble (either not being able to sleep or sleeping too much)
- eating trouble (not eating or eating too much)
- cutting, or other ways of physically hurting oneself
- increased use of drugs or alcohol
- thoughts or discussions of suicide

Getting Help

People with mood disorders who don't want or can't take psychiatric medicine can try alternative therapies. These are treatments used *instead of* drugs. One of the most common alternative therapies is light therapy.

Light Therapy

Have you ever noticed how different you can feel depending on the weather? On bright, sunny days we often feel hopeful, energetic, and positive. On cloudy, rainy days we tend to feel more tired and glum. Our different moods are often the result of differences in amount of light we receive. In his work *Beyond Prozac*, Dr. Michael J. Norden notes that light affects serotonin levels: more light causes serotonin levels to go up; less light causes them to go down. If low brain serotonin levels cause us to feel more irritable, less energetic, and less able to sleep (all symptoms of depression), then an increase in serotonin levels should bring relief to those symptoms. One way to increase serotonin without drugs is to use light therapy.

Light therapy, or phototherapy as it is sometimes called, involves having a patient sit in front of a specially designed light—not an ordinary light like you find at home; it must be much brighter and

Most people feel happier and more energetic on bright, sunny days. Light therapy uses a very bright light to simulate the effect of the sun.

more intense. The recommended brightness of a phototherapy light is ten thousand lux—approximately twenty times brighter than your average living room lamp lightbulb.

Lights used in light therapy are designed to be easy to use. They often come in the shape of a large rectangular box about two feet long, one foot high, and three inches deep (although new designs include desk lights and visors). High-intensity lightbulbs are set inside the box behind an opaque screen (called a diffuser) that protects the patient from dangerous ultraviolet rays and glare. The box can be put on a tabletop as it is or can be attached to a special frame to tilt the light at an angle more like that of the sun's rays.

For light therapy to be effective, the patient must sit close to the box (usually within twenty inches) and spend a regular amount of time in front of it each day (fifteen minutes to two hours). This treatment is especially effective for people who suffer from seasonal affective disorder (SAD), particularly if they start light therapy in the fall and continue it through the winter and early spring.

Light therapy helps three out of four people with SAD. It is a highly effective therapy with very few side effects. (The primary one is eye strain from the light's brightness.) Light therapy is a safe alternative to drug treatment for people with depression (especially SAD), but is also used in combination with drug therapies.

While light therapy is a great alternative, it's not the only choice. Some choose "natural" drugs instead.

Chapter 7

Drowning

shley never guessed that just seven days after her near overdose she would again brush up against death; no warning signs hinted at the tragedy poised to strike.

Her first week out of the hospital wasn't as bad as Ashley had feared. Few students at Marina High commented on her behavior at the party, and Ashley kept busy by visiting Dr. Graham twice and attending an Alateen meeting. She continued to feel sad or anxious at times, but overall, it was not a bad week.

Ashley realized Dr. Graham was right: she was improving. Entire days still went by when she seemed emotionally washed out, but Dr. Graham was helping Ashley become more aware of her emotions. Now, she could label and counter feelings of fear, distrust, or anxiety. Her mood disorder seemed less like some terrible monster enslaving her and more like a tamed beast that she could talk to and control.

By Saturday, Ashley felt able to look for another job. She knew she would need to work soon, especially with the semester nearing its end, and she felt strong enough to cope with employment again. She put in applications at several tourist shops lining Main Street, as well as the Surf and Sport and Quicksilver stores.

No one appeared to be hiring, so the attempt to find a job left Ashley feeling somewhat diminished. She headed for the Java Coffee Shop, thinking a hot cup of espresso would lift her spirits.

She stopped short at the store entrance. Vanna and a group of her friends were there. *Yuck*, thought Ashley, *I don't need to hear her now.*

Feeling lonely, she drifted back toward her car in the public parking lot by the pier. On the way, she tried to call Josh, but his mom said he had left early in the morning and she didn't know where he might be. Ashley drove home. Maybe she would sit and watch television with her father, try bonding with him a little bit that way. Unfortunately, she found him on the roof repairing shingles, and he didn't have time to chat.

She felt the old sadness creeping in, but she was determined to do something more than lie around and feel bad. Going to the garage, Ashley took her surfboard off the wall, a beauty, nine feet long with a huge old-school single fin, custom made by Harbor Surf Shop. She lashed the board on the rack atop her Corolla and headed down the coast.

An hour later, Ashley was far out from shore, straddling her board and looking out to sea. She had caught a good set of waves soon after hitting the water, zigzagging on the lips of three- and four-foot swells, feeling the old exhilaration again. But then the ocean went flat. She paddled farther out to sea, but it remained frustratingly calm. She lay back on her board, her eyes closed against the harsh glare of the sun.

She wondered why was everything so hard in her life? She knew Dr. Graham would say she was playing "the old negative tapes" in her head; she should try to reverse the "downward spiral" of these unhealthy thoughts.

Ashley was pulled away from her musings by a thunderous roar. She glanced toward the horizon, and then she sat up.

The biggest wave she had ever seen, a huge wall of water, was racing toward her. She had drifted parallel to the wave, a dangerous position. Desperately, Ashley tried to turn the board in line with the rushing wall of water, but she didn't have time to complete the maneuver. She took a fast breath and rolled the board upside down a moment before the liquid avalanche overtook her.

The next moment, she felt the board torn away from her hands. Astonished, she watched it fly away from her sight, leaving her stuck in an underwater circular current. Round and round she spun in a series of submerged summersaults. Dimly, she realized that the leash that attached her board to her ankle had broken.

Ashley fought to reach the surface. Finally, she popped up into the air, coughed, spat, and opened her mouth for a deep breath . . . just as the next wave smashed down on her. Brine gushed down her throat as the undercurrent dragged her downward like a pair of enormous hands. No matter how hard she thrashed against the undercurrent, she could not resist its force pulling her under.

Was this the way her life was going to end? Maybe it wasn't so bad after all—no more struggling to be happy. Funny: this was the way Stacie had died, not far from here. They had been so close in life; now they would be united in death. Ashley quit struggling; she would just let the ocean take her . . . take her from this life . . . take her to a place where she could be free from all worry.

And then, something inside her screamed: *NO! I WANT TO LIVE!* It was a revelation, a moment of absolute certainty. Kicking and stroking with all her might, she pulled herself atop the water and gasped for breath. She glanced toward the shore and began to crawl toward it, but the current was pulling her out to sea. The huge waves were creating a massive undertow—a riptide!

Ashley tried to swim sideways, to find a way out of the oceanward current, but it was too strong. Her muscles were aching; her arms and legs felt as though they were on fire. Then the next wave hit; again she was tumbled under the water, and she couldn't hold her breath long enough to surface. Again, her lungs filled with water.

She was losing feeling in her extremities, her limbs turning to jelly. How ironic, mused a small, distant piece of her brain, she couldn't remember a time when she had wanted more desperately to remain alive, but now she was drowning. Her mind called out a desperate prayer: *I want to live!*

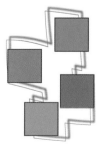

Depression leads people to focus mostly on failures and disappointments, to emphasize the negative side of their situations, and to downplay their own capabilities or worth. Depression affects a person's thoughts so that the individual fails to see possible solutions to her dilemma. A teen with depression may feel like there's no other way out of problems, no other escape from emotional pain, or no other way to communicate his desperate unhappiness.

When depression lifts because a person gets the proper therapy or treatment, the distorted thinking is cleared. The person can find pleasure, energy, and hope again.

Other Treatments for Moods Herbs and Vitamins

If you are considering taking herbal or vitamin supplements instead of FDA-approved prescription drugs to treat your mood disorder or its symptoms, remember two things:

1. Herbs and vitamins are chemicals, and chemicals *are* drugs. Any chemical you put into your body can alter the way you think, act, or feel. Just because a chemical takes the form of an herb or vitamin doesn't mean it is not a drug. And, since herbs and vitamins are drugs, they can (and will) cause side effects.

2. Herbs and vitamins are **not** regulated by the FDA. That means that one brand of St. John's wort might have far more active ingredients in each pill than another. With "natural" drugs, it's harder to be sure of what you're getting

and how much to take. You'll have to watch carefully that you don't take too much.

If someone is still interested in using herbs to treat depression or anxiety, she should always consult her doctor first. Here are some options she might want to discuss with him:

- St. John's wort (also called Hypericum perforatum) relieves mild depression.
- Ginkgo biloba improves memory by increasing blood flow to brain.
- Hops has a calming effect and makes you sleepy.

Consult your doctor before taking any herbal remedies for depression. Herbs and vitamins are chemicals that are not regulated by the FDA and so should be taken carefully.

- Kava reduces anxiety.
- Caffeine improves mood.
- Melatonin (a hormone) improves memory and helps you sleep.

Many people with depression and anxiety, especially Europeans, report being helped by these alternatives. But these substances, except for hops, also cause side effects.

- St. John's wort can cause sensitivity to sunlight, dry mouth, upset stomach, dizziness, and diarrhea.

- Ginkgo biloba can cause upset stomach, dizziness, headaches, and allergic reactions.

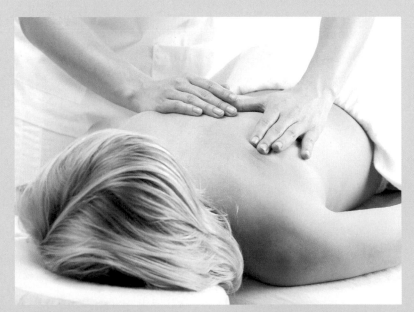

Massage therapy is an alternative form of treatment for anxiety and depression.

- Kava, after large doses, can cause muscle spasms, shortness of breath, and yellow skin.

- Caffeine use can lead to addiction, "the jitters," sleep problems, restlessness; withdrawal from caffeine can cause depressed mood, headache, and irritability.

- Melatonin can cause light sensitivity.

As with any drugs these remedies can interact with routine medications (including cold or cough syrups, pain relievers, and allergy medications) and could cause potentially dangerous side effects when taken with other drugs.

Other Alternatives

People with anxiety and depression have a host of other treatment options from which to choose: diet and dietary supplements (what you eat can affect how you feel); electroconvulsive therapy (ECT; this is a safe, painless treatment today); acupuncture (the ancient Chinese practice of inserting tiny needles into certain pressure points, which is reported to work as well as drug treatment with fewer side effects); aromatherapy (using scented oils to trigger emotional responses); massage therapy (total body massage to cause deep muscle relaxation); and meditation and relaxation techniques.

Chapter 8
New Beginnings

shley lay on the sand, retching and twitching. Five lifeguards in their red outfits squatted around her, monitoring her vital signs. A crowd of onlookers stood outside the guards, curious to see a real rescue scene. Ashley wasn't bothered by the uninvited attention. She was alive! The sun had never seemed so bright, the warm sand never felt so good. *Thank heavens for good timing.* A patrol boat had come by and spotted her just in the nick of time.

"Hey! Let me through, she's my friend!" Ashley squinted against the sun and saw . . . Josh! The tall boy pushed his way into the ring of lifeguards and dropped onto his knees. "Ashley, are you all right?"

She flashed an exhausted smile at her friend. "Never been better, Josh. Yourself?"

Relief washed across his face.

Fifteen minutes later, the lifeguards declared her to be in stable condition. Ashley stood on her exhausted legs, thanked the guards profusely, and walked to a bench. She and Josh sat watching skaters and bikers zoom past them.

Josh shook his head. "Ashley, I was so scared. I saw the guards bring someone in, and I thought, 'Hope the poor girl is all right,' and then I saw that it was *you* and I just freaked. I was so scared!"

"Yeah, you and me both—it was pretty scary."

Josh paused a moment and looked uncomfortable Ashley guessed what he was going to say next. "Ashley, you weren't trying to drown yourself, were you?"

Ashley shook her head vehemently. "No, Josh, I did not try to kill myself. My leash broke, the wave took my board, and then I was in this nasty riptide. I swear, Josh, I never realized how much I want to *live* before today."

Josh smiled. "Yeah, sometimes you don't realize how much something means to you, until someone tries to take it away."

Ashley nodded. "I've been given a second chance. I know life won't ever be perfect, and I'll probably always have to work with my depression and anxiety problems, but I'm never going to take my life for granted again."

They paused to watch a funky-looking Rasta man go by on rollerblades, strumming a guitar. They both smiled.

"Hey," Josh said, "What do you do for fun the night after you almost drown?"

"I dunno," Ashley replied. "Is this a joke?"

"Naw, I was wondering if you wanted to have dinner and see a movie with me?"

Ashley looked at him, her eyebrows raised. "Josh, are you asking me out on a date?"

Josh grinned back at her. "Yeah, I guess so. What do you say?"

Ashley looked down at the ground. "I don't know Josh. I mean, I really like you. . . . But I'm scared. I'm such a freaking mess, I'm afraid that I'll just complicate your life with my issues."

Josh's grin didn't fade. "Well gee, Ashley, I guess I'll just have to wait until I meet the perfect girl, without any problems. Where should I look for someone like that? Maybe I should date one of the mannequins in the bikini shop window."

"Josh, I'm serious."

"So am I, Ashley. You're great; you're honest and creative; and you're not superficial like most of the girls at Marina High are. No one is perfect, and no matter how messed up you feel, I like being with you. So what do you say? Want to see a movie?"

"I'd love to go out with you, Josh!" She took his hand, noting how small her own thin fingers looked twining around his. "But first I have to go do something."

"Okay," he said. "Pick you up at eight?"

"Yeah. That's awesome. I'll see you then."

She gave him a smile and walked toward her Toyota. Then she drove up the coast and turned inland, stopping at a convenience store to buy a bouquet of flowers before driving up a winding road past grass-covered hills. She drove through the entrance of Shepherd's Rest Cemetery and stopped her car beside a familiar marker.

As she arranged the flowers carefully in front of Stacie's tombstone, she whispered to her friend, "Stacie, I'll always miss you—but I realize now that you and I have different destinies. This is how you found freedom, but I'm going to find freedom from my depression in this life. From now on I'm going to try to live every day to its fullest . . . for both of us."

Ashley stood and stared toward the orange disk of the sun disappearing below the golden hillsides. She had better start back; there would be just enough time to get home and change her clothes before Josh arrived.

Unfortunately, teens are vulnerable to anxiety and depression. Adolescence is a time in life when many people must learn how to handle new challenges and stresses in the world around them. At the same time, the world inside them—their own hormones, brains, and sleep cycles—is also changing radically, and these physical changes can affect mood as well. But depression and anxiety don't have to control a teen's life.

If you (or someone you know) is coping with depression or anxiety, remember, how to treat your anxiety or depression is a deeply personal choice, one that should involve the individual, the family, and a mental health professional. With the number of options available today, everyone should be able to find a treatment strategy that works.

A person beginning treatment needs to remember that she will have good days and bad days. Overcoming depression or anxiety takes time. If one treatment option doesn't work, he should try another. Loved ones can help as well. When they receive love, support, and understanding, along with the proper medical treatment, most people with depression or anxiety can overcome their overwhelming emotions— or at least learn to live successfully with them. In either case, it takes great courage to risk treatment and change—but when people with depression or anxiety are willing to take the risk, and get the help and support they need, they can lead happy, fulfilled lives.

Moods do not need to rule a person's life. There is hope and help available—and the outlook is good for full recovery.

Glossary

antidote: A substance that counteracts the effects of a toxin or poison.

apathy: The lack of interest in anything.

chronic: Long term or recurring frequently.

cognitive: Relating to the process of acquiring knowledge.

Cushing's disease: A disorder caused by the excessive production of the hormone ACTH by the pituitary gland.

dopamine: A chemical compound found in the brain that transmits nerve impulses.

fluctuate: Change levels.

hypoglycemia: A medical condition in which there is too little sugar in the blood.

hypothyroidism: The medical condition caused by a deficiency in the production of thyroid hormones produced by the thyroid glands.

inarticulate: Unable to express oneself well or understandably.

incapacitating: Making someone or something powerless or ineffective.

maladaptive: Unsuitable for a particular situation, function, or purpose.

mood disorder: A psychological condition caused by abnormalities in emotional states.

norepinephrine: A hormone secreted by the adrenal gland that is the principal neurotransmitter of the sympathetic nerve endings supplying the major organs and skin.

organic: Relating to a bodily organ or affecting the basic structure of the organism.

Parkinson's disease: An incurable nervous disorder characterized by trembling hands, lifeless face, monotone voice, and a slow, shuffling walk.

pessimistic: Having a negative attitude.

physiological: Relating to the way living things function.

prevalent: Widely found.

psychoanalysis: A psychology theory based on the idea that mental life functions on both conscious and unconscious levels.

seizures: Sudden attacks; the physical manifestations (as convulsions, sensory disturbances, or loss of consciousness) resulting from abnormal electrical discharges in the brain.

startle response: The emotional, behavioral, and physiological response to an unexpected, sudden stimulus.

traumatic: Extremely distressing, frightening, or shocking, sometimes with long-term psychological effects.

twin studies: Research conducted on twins, with one acting as the control.

Further Reading

Amen, Daniel G. *Healing Anxiety and Depression.* Los Angeles: Berkeley, 2004.

Bornstein, Kate. *Hello, Cruel World: 101 Alternatives to Suicide for Teens, Freaks and Other Outlaws.* New York: Seven Stories, 2006.

Copeland, Mary Ellen. *Recovering from Depression: A Workbook for Teens.* New York: Brookes, 2002.

Crook, Marion. *Out of the Darkness: Teens Talk About Suicide.* New York: Arsenal, 2004.

Empfield, Maureen. *Understanding Teenage Depression: A Guide to Diagnosis, Treatment, and Management.* New York: Owl Books, 2001.

Koplewicz, Harold. *More Than Moody.* New York: Perigree, 2004.

Nelson, Richard E. *The Power to Prevent Suicide: A Guide for Teens Helping Teens.* New York: Free Spirit, 2006.

Schab, Lisa. *The Anxiety Workbook for Teens.* New York: Instant Help, 2005.

Seaward, Brian. *Hot Stones and Funny Bones: Teens Helping Teens Cope with Stress.* New York: HCI, 2002.

Welch, Edward T. *Depression: The Way Up When You Are Down.* Phillipsburg, N.J.: P & R Publishing, 2000.

Publisher's note:
The Web sites listed on the following page were active at the time of publication. The publisher is not responsible for Web sites that have changed their addresses or discontinued operation since the date of publication. The publisher will review and update the Web-site list upon each reprint.

For More Information

American Psychological Association
750 First Street, N.E.
Washington, DC 20002
www.apa.org

American Psychiatric Association
1400 K St., N.W.
Washington, DC 20005
www.psych.org

Anxiety Disorders Association of America
www.adaa.org

Coping with Adolescent Depression and Suicide
(Oregon DHS)
www.dhs.state.or.us/publichealth/ipe/docs/coping.cfm

Depression and Teens
www.depressedteens.com/indexfl.html

My Friend Is Talking About Suicide. What Should I Do?
(KidsHealth)
www.kidshealth.org/teen/your_mind/problems/talking_
about_suicide.html

National Anxiety Foundation
www.lexington-on-line.com/haf.html

National Mental Health Association
1021 Prince Street
Alexandria, VA 22314-2971
www.nmha.org

Suicide Prevention—Depression and Bipolar Support
Alliance
www.dbsalliance.org/info/suicide.html

Bibliography

American Society of Clinical Psychopharmacology, Inc. Depression.org. http://www.depression.org.

"Clinical Depression: What You Need to Know." National Mental Health Association. http://www.nmha.org/infoctr/factsheets/21.cfm.

Depression.com. http://www.depression.com.

DRADA: Depression and Related Affective Disorders Association. http://www.drada.org/Facts/childandadolescent.html.

Green, W. H. *Child and Adolescent Clinical Psychopharmacology*. Philadelphia: Lippincott Williams & Wilkins, 2001.

"In Harms Way: Suicide in America." National Institute of Mental Health. http://www.nimh.nih.gov/publicat/harmaway.cfm.

Harwitz, D., and L. Ravizza. "Suicide and depression." *Emergency Medicine Clinic of North America* 18(May 2000): 263–271.

Hayward C., J. D. Killen, and H. C. Kraemer. "Predictors of panic attacks in adolescents." Journal of American Academy of Child and Adolescent Psychiatry 39(February 2000): 207–214.

Osvath, P., V. Voros, and S. Fekete. "Life events and psychopathology in a group of suicide attempters." *Psychopathology* 37(January–February 2004): 36–40.

"Teen Suicide." American Academy of Child & Adolescent Psychiatry. http://www.aacap.org/publications/factsfam/suicide.htm.

Teenshealth: Suicide http://www.kidshealth.org/teen/your_mind/mental_health/suicide.htm.

Index

acupuncture 113
agoraphobia 34, 35
antianxiety medications
68–69
    alternatives to 76-77
    risks of 70
    side effects of 72–73
antidepressants 67–68
    alternatives to 76–77
    risks of 70
    side effects of 70–71
anxiety
    alternative treatments
        110–113
    benefit of 19–20
    causes of 86–88
    definition 18–21
    diagnosis of 91–92
    disorders 21
    medications 68–69
    symptoms 21
    treatment 67–77
    who affected 47–48

benzodiazepines 69, 72
brain 15, 16, 53 –57

caffeine 112, 113

depression
    alternative treatments
        110–113
    causes 49–53
    definition 16–18
    diagnosis of 88–90
    medications 67–68

    symptoms 16–17
    treatment 67–77
    warning signs 89–90
    who affected 46–47

electroconvulsive therapy
(ECT) 113
exercise 76–77

"fight-or-flight" 19, 87–88
Freud, Sigmund 86

Generalized Anxiety
Disorder (GAD) 30–31
ginkgo biloba 110, 112

herbs 110–113
hops 111

kava 112, 113

light therapy 101–103

massage therapy 113
melatonin 112, 113
monoamine oxidase
inhibitors (MAOIs) 67, 71
mood disorder
    definition 16
    types of 16–19, 30–37
moods 15, 16

National Institute of Mental
Health (NIMH) 46
neurotransmitters 54–56, 57
nerve cells 53, 54, 56, 57

panic attack with
agoraphobia 34–35
panic disorder
    definition 31
    effects of 32–34
    symptoms 31–32
phobia
    definition 35
    social 37
    types of 35–36
psychoanalysis 86

selective serotonin reuptake
inhibitors (SSRIs) 67, 70,
71
St. John's wort 111, 112

suicide 99–101
synapse 54, 55

therapy
    behavioral 75
    cognitive 75
    interpersonal 75
    psychodynamic 76
    supportive 74–75
    who is qualified 73–74
tricyclic antidepressants 67

ventromedial prefrontal
cortex 16
vitamins 110

Picture Credits

fotolia.com
      Blazic, Ana: p. 31
      Brzozowski, Rados: p. 48
      Faull, Thomas: p. 89
      Sommer, John: p. 34
      Toscani, Paolo: p. 52
      Voznjuk, Andrey: p. 91
      Wackerhausen, Jacob: p. 102
      Zagorski, Mateusz: p. 68
istockphoto
      Balcerzak, Marcin: p. 71
      Crockett, David: p. 111
      DlGlcal: p. 51
      Kaulitzki, Sebastian: p. 55
Jupiter Images: pp. 15, 17, 19, 20, 33, 46, 50, 71, 87, 100, 113
Library of Congress: p. 86

To the best knowledge of the publisher, all other images are in the public domain. If any image has been inadvertently uncredited, please notify Harding House Publishing Service, Vestal, New York 13850, so that rectification can be made for future printings.

Authors

Kenneth McIntosh is a freelance writer living in northern Arizona with his family. He has written two dozen educational books, and taught at junior high, high school, and community college levels.

Phyllis Livingston has her master's degree in special education. She has worked with a wide variety of teenagers with various psychiatric disorders, including depression and anxiety.

Series Consultants

Sharon Levy, MD, MPH received her MD from New York University School of Medicine and completed her residency at NYU Med Ctr/Bellevue Hospital. She was later awarded a Dyson Fellowship at Children's Hospital Boston. She currently works as an Assistant in Medicine in the General Pediatrics department of the Children's Hospital Boston (CHB), where she also is director of the Adolescent Substance Abuse Program (ASAP). In addition, Dr. Levy serves as an instructor in Pediatrics for Harvard Medical School. Dr. Levy's research focuses on development of drug use treatment strategies for adolescent patients that can be used in the ambulatory medical setting. In previous work she examined physicians' knowledge, practices and attitudes regarding drug testing of adolescent patients and the use of home drug testing by parents of adolescent children.

Cindy Croft, M.A.Ed., is the Director of the Center for Inclusive Child Care (CICC) at Concordia University, St. Paul, MN. The CICC is a comprehensive resource network for promoting and supporting inclusive early childhood and school-age programs and providers with Project EXCEPTIONAL training and consultation, and other resources at www.inclusivechildcare. org. In addition to working with the CICC, Ms. Croft is on the faculty at Concordia University and Minneapolis Community and Technical College.